BUDS AND SCUDS

NOBODY'S A NOTHIN' BOOK 2

PAUL MAITLAND

BUDS AND SCUDS: Nobody's a Nothin' Book Two
©2024 by PAUL MAITLAND
All rights reserved.

ISBN-13: 979-8-9890806-8-7
Also available in eBook

Little Roni Publishers
ALABAMA | TENNESSEE
www.littleronipublishers.com
V12042024SC

For Shirley

Just in case, you know, you want to know about how Zip got into cross country running, and how he met the Buds, and how he was thrown into the pond by the Scuds and completely soaked his school books and tennis shoes...

I mean, go on, if you want to.

But if you want to read Book 1 first, it's on Amazon.com.

Go ahead, we'll wait. I bet you'll love it!

PART I: WATERLOO

If you hate history, you may want to skip to page 3.

Sarah loves literature, Hu loves science, and I love history. Maybe someday we can start a school for kids who love to read.

Napoleon Bonaparte is a semi-hero of mine because he was a pipsqueak (some say five-foot-two, taller than I am), but also a winner.

Well, until he was a loser, that is.

Napoleon made lieutenant in the French army at sixteen years old, joined the French Revolution, was second in command of the army by age twenty-six, seized power in France at thirty, and at thirty-five crowned himself Emperor of the French. A military genius, he conquered most of Europe, destroyed the last vestiges of feudalism, instituted reforms including the Napoleonic Code of laws which France still follows, and reformed a whole continent. His military strategies are still studied today. He was very popular with the ordinary people.

But then…

But then, he got big-headed and selfish. He lost the support of his people and was defeated by the British Duke of Wellington at Waterloo. He died a loser in exile on an island near Italy.

Napoleon had his Waterloo; I had my Farraday. I was feeling pretty good about myself. How was I to know the fat hand of fate was about to fall on me?

I should have known.

It was April Fools' Day.

1

GUESS WHAT?

You can't always be the winner.

Fathers have favorite sayings. You don't ever forget them, not because they are clever, but because fathers never stop saying them. The *winner* thing is one of my dad's. So is, *Honesty is the ONLY policy.*

I try to live up to his sayings; really, I do.

๑๑๑

Strolling down the halls of Hanway Middle School, I felt content. Winning last fall's cross country championship had earned me a bit of respect. I had friends now. My sworn enemies, the Scuds, were too busy with their candy smuggling business to notice me. In fact, I'd started admiring their smooth operation.

The Scuds were strutting in front of me, doing business. A kid, coming from the opposite direction, would high-five two dollars into the paw of Booger Schmidt and keep walking, then Noford Hammond would come along, reach into the bulging pockets of his huge cargo pants, grab a PayDay (or whatever), and low-five it into the customer's hand.

My mind was occupied trying to invent an April Fools' joke to play on my friends, the Buds. Turns out, I was the April fool.

Just as Billy Jean Bogarde slipped Booger two bills, the principal's door opened. Noford already had a Twix in his hand. To get rid of it, he flicked it backward. My reflexes are excellent. Without thinking I caught it.

"Hands up!" shrieked Principal Farraday.

Every hand in the hallway flew skyward, including mine. Everyone sucked in the school air before I did. When I tried to breathe, none was left. The principal yanked his hook into me and reeled me in to his office.

This was my third time this school year.

Three strikes, you're out.

"What is this?' he demanded, pulling my arm down in front of me.

"Twix, sir," I answered.

"Perhaps you could expound on how you procured this poison!"

"I d-d-don't understand, sir."

"You don't understand?" He fired the candy into the waste

can. "Preposterous. Possession of this property is proof-positive of your perfidy."

Yeesh. This must be "p" week in his project of memorizing the dictionary.

"Perplexing, it is, that peons such as you propound such plots. Your name is?"

I wanted to say Noford Hammond but knew better. "Corey Zilch."

"Zilch, yes, I place you now. You possess a propensity for problematic performance."

Oh, boy. Nobody wants to be remembered by the principal. "I'm innocent, sir. The Twix flew in my face."

"Propelled from where? A pawn, are you? Then who is your provider? Who are the primary participants?"

Easy for him to say. If I ratted out the Scuds, I would never have peace again, inside or out of school.

How can I pull myself out of this precarious predicament?

Yeesh, now I was thinking like him.

"Please, it was an accident. Somebody saw you and threw the candy at me. Everyone is afraid of you, sir."

A smile of satisfaction crossed his face. "Zilch, here is my proposition. You are on parole with one proviso. You will position yourself to penetrate the perimeter of the perpetrators and periodically report to me."

Oh, great, Corey Zilch the Snitch, just what I wanted to be. But I had no choice. The principal could suspend me for having candy, or even send me to Juvie like he did Amy last year. I said, "Everyone saw you pull me in, so if you don't punish me some way, they'll know I am spying for you."

"Point well taken, my boy. Possession, then, will be punishable by no participation in spring sports."

As I trudged to the door, I saw Principal Farraday reaching into the waste can.

Candy smuggling is profitable at Hanway School. The government of our nation has declared we children will be healthy even if it kills us. Our school has been chosen as the perfect laboratory.

When it was announced the spokesperson said, "If it can work in the backwater of America, it can work anywhere."

So, the only kind of food available in our school is the "healthy" stuff, approved by Washington, D. C., and eaten by no kid in his or her right mind. No bag lunches, no cookies, no soda, not even a cough drop, is allowed. Therefore, smuggled candy makes big money.

The rest of the school day was a blur. I never saw my old friends or my new ones.

Although I usually ran the trail at Butterworth Park after school, this day I just wanted to run home to my room. I dragged myself to the corner of the schoolyard, where the clump of lilac bushes borders the football field. The lilacs, just budding, couldn't hide human figures lurking there. Was it the Scuds lying in wait to beat me up again? I didn't care. My life was over anyway. I'd just had a birthday. I guess thirteen really is an unlucky number.

Two figures sprang out in front of me—one tall redhead, pretty, one short boy, not pretty—Sarah and Hu. I could breathe again.

"We need to talk," they said.

"April fools?"

"No. Serious talk."

I didn't feel like talking, so I turned to go the other way. Two others stood there, tall and blond, my cross country teammate, Harley, and his sister Justine.

Harley said, "Don't bother to run, Zip. You know I can outrun you."

That was true.

Justine added, "I can, too."

"No, you can't."

"She might," said Harley.

The four of them linked hands around me, making me the monkey in the middle, and ushered me over to the grandstands. This had all the markings of an intervention.

Sarah started with, "We don't like how you've changed, Corey. You've gotten a big head. We liked the small-headed Corey better."

"The old Corey was a nothing," I said. "Now I'm Zip Zilch. I'm a something!"

"You're a something, all right," she responded, "but being something involves accepting responsibility for your commitments, and you're neglecting yours."

Hu chimed in with, "Do you remember our oath—*Buds forever, loyal and true?*"

"Huh?"

"You seem to be more loyal to the Studs than to the Buds."

"Who are the Studs?"

"The sports guys, you dork. You've been eating lunch with them."

"They're good guys. You're one of them, Harley. So is Jimmy Smithers. Nice guys."

"Sure," said Harley, "nice and shallow. All we talk about is sports, cars, and girls. I'm sick of it."

"Sick of sports, cars, and girls?"

"No, sick of being shallow. I want more. You talk about science and history and poetry and other important things I want to learn about. Since Justine's been hanging with you guys, I've been kind of jealous that she has friends like you."

"You're an eighth grader and a jock. You're jealous of us?"

He hung his lower lip, slack-jawed, crossed his eyes, and picked his nose. "Ya know, I h'aint just no purty face."

They all had a good laugh together.

"Here's the deal, Corey," Sarah declared. "You can't be both a Bud and a Stud. If you give up the Studs, Harley will come with you, at least until he graduates in two months. That will make the Buds five strong."

"What about Jimmy?" I asked. "He's a Stud."

"That's up to him," Harley answered.

Hu said, "There's more. You give up the big head you got for winning one race last fall. Big heads don't look good on little guys like us."

I should have agreed right away, but I liked the status of being a Stud. Instead, I said, "I'll think about it."

As I slunk away Justine yelled back, "Don't think too long!"

ΩΩΩ

I am just under five feet tall, a shrimp for sure, but with this new load on my shoulders I felt smaller yet. I practically crawled home. Dragging up the driveway, head down, I heard a cheerful voice exclaim, "Welcome home, son!"

I lifted my gaze. What to my wondering eyes should appear but my overweight father in orange running gear.

"Corey, I've decided you shouldn't have to run alone, so I've decided to go to work earlier every morning. That way I can be at home by four-thirty to run with you. We'll have a great time together, male bonding and all."

Yeesh! I would have no choice but to run through the neighborhood with him.

My dad was so out of shape, we didn't actually run. We jogged. We stopped for him to catch his breath. We jogged again. Three blocks shouldn't take half an hour. All the neighbors came to their windows to ogle us—Linus and the Great Pumpkin.

Three humiliations in one day, and you are definitely *out!*

At five o'clock, inside the front door, between panting and moaning, my dad announced, "Just wait until supper time. I have a surprise for you."

Oh, boy. What else?

ℚℚℚ

As we sat down to enjoy our great American supper of goulash, sauerkraut, and garlic bread, Dad handed me a BiggyMart bag.

"For you, my boy. Open it." I did, and my fears came true. I pulled out a neon orange sweat suit. Dad grinned. "Now we can match."

Well, at least this should be the worst of it.

That's when Mom spoke up. "Guess what?"

2

MINI-ME

Before I tell you what "what" meant, I need to bring you up to speed.

One cross country race shouldn't shake the world, but the conference championship race I won in the fall of seventh grade shook mine. My first ever cross country success changed me, some for the better and some for the worse. The big surprise was the way it shook up my family.

My father finally noticed me. Sarah says he had an *epiphany*. Hu says the fathering gene awoke from hibernation, stumbled from its cave, and began to roar. For twelve years, our home was dull and uncomplicated. Suddenly my dad wanted to be involved in my life, and at the same time my mom became very interested in my sister.

On the day of the race last fall, to celebrate *our* winning the conference cross country meet, Dad took our whole family to my favorite restaurant, The Rusty Sword. He even invited Jimmy Smithers, Sis's newly discovered boyfriend, to join the party. We ate *crocodile jaws* (chicken wings), *doubloons* (round-sliced, deep-fried potatoes), and *walk-the-planks* (fried mozzarella sticks). We each drank *a bottle of rum* (root beer),

10

and for dessert we all *sailed the seven c's* (chocolate-chip-coconut-cream-custard-with-cookie-crust pie).

Avast, me hardies! 'Twas a meal unfit for Hanway!

While Dad interrogated Jimmy and Mom quizzed Sis about "how long has this been going on," I was alone with my thoughts. I replayed in my head the whole race, sealing every detail forever in my memory in case it was the only victory I ever won. When my inner video ended, I raised my arms in triumph, and yelled, "Yes!"

They all turned and stared.

"I won!"

"You won, Zip!" Jimmy agreed.

"We saw," said Sis.

The Rusty Sword gives you a plastic, rust-colored sword as a knife, a trident for a fork, and a peg-leg-handled spoon. My sister's usual way of eating here is to stab a croc with her sword, jab several doubloons with her trident, and alternate bites. This time she glared at me, bit with a vengeance, chewed noisily, and swallowed with a dramatic gulp.

Jimmy seemed to find this attractive. Whenever her sword or trident went empty, she pointed it at me and growled, "A-r-r-r-gh!" Jimmy only grinned.

When we had dropped Jimmy off at his house and arrived at ours, Sis went to her room and slammed the door. Mom went to her room and locked herself in. Dad disappeared into the garage.

I sat alone with my thoughts. I replayed the race and raised my arms high at the finish line. Then, in the quiet, I heard crying from Mom's room. After listening a minute at the door, I tiptoed to Sis's room, knocked, and said, "Mom's crying."

"Go away!"

I went away.

After a while, Sis emerged and motioned me over. She knocked on Mom's door, and asked, "Can we come in?" Mom unlocked the door to let us in.

"Did I do something wrong?" I asked.

"No, baby, you did something right."

Sis said, "Then it was me. What did I do?"

"Nothing, honey. You both did right. I was wrong. I tried to keep you babies, and you both grew up on me on the same day."

Mom bawled, Sis hugged her and bawled, and I went away.

Dad entered from the garage, arms loaded with a hockey stick, a basketball, a football, a volleyball, and a hand pump. He lined them up in the front hallway, looked up at me about to speak, but I beat him to it.

"Mom and Sis are crying."

"Oh, boy," he said and went back to the garage.

When he returned, he had a basketball hoop and net, a volleyball net, a football helmet, and a hockey puck. He opened his mouth to speak, but at that moment Sis snuck out of Mom's bedroom, grabbed a box of tissues from the coffee table, and headed to her own room. Mom motioned to Dad from the doorway. Dad took a deep breath and shuffled over to her like he was going to the guillotine. They disappeared into their bedroom and never came out.

After a while, I showered and went to bed, but I couldn't figure out what I was supposed to cry about.

ooo

Everything was okay that Sunday morning, just different. Dad was not in his pajamas in the living room, but in his U-of-I sweatshirt in the front hallway, and instead of reading the Sunday paper he was pumping air into the football. Mom and Sis were yakking in the kitchen. I was still trying to figure out what was going on.

"Breakfast is ready," Mom announced. At last, something normal—scrambled eggs, bacon, and toast. Normal food tastes wonderful; or it did, until Mom said, "Sis made it!"

I couldn't un-eat it, could I? I hoped for the best.

We watched the humpbacked preacher from Texas, as usual, but when the "everybody-fall-down" guy came on, Mom and Sis went back to the kitchen to work on dinner. I helped Dad pump up dead balls, wipe cobwebs off sports equipment, and douse it all with Lysol.

Our All-American Sunday dinner turned Chinese—beef and broccoli over fried rice. Used to be that Dad didn't talk until his stomach was happy, but in a remarkable reversal of fate, after just one bite, he said, "Very good! What a great meal for your first day as a cook!"

Being hungry, I ate it anyway.

After Sunday dinners in November, Dad had always watched football, but this time he decided to play football with me. He tried his high school helmet on my head.

It fell off.

He tried it on his head.

It was too small.

He showed me how to throw a football, fingers on the stitches, hand cocked behind the head, straight toward the target, fingers rolling off the seam.

My hand was too small. When I cocked my arm, the ball fell in the grass behind me.

Dad demonstrated a perfect spiral pass right to my chest. The ball knocked me flat, leaving a perfect purple raspberry.

All winter was the same. Now that Dad had an athlete to work with, he was determined to turn Zip Zilch into his Mini-

Me. Now that Mom had a *woman* to work with, she was going to make Sis into her Mini-Mom, even though Sis was already taller than my mother.

I kept running, the one sport I was good at, and I tried my best to satisfy my dad—or at least to entertain him.

Which brings us back to the disaster of April Fools' Day.

3

PARENTHOOD

om said, "Guess what?"

I'd not heard those words since last year when she announced she and Sis were going to be on TV with the First Lady. This had to be big.

Sis and I spoke at the same time. "What?"

Dad grinned. "Your mother and I have talked it over, and we've made a decision."

Yeesh. We were moving to Alaska to live with the polar bears. Or maybe Dad was quitting his job to join the circus as a trapeze artist. Or Mom was turning our house into a bed-and-breakfast, and I would be living in the basement with the mice. Turns out, that last one was close, but not as bad as what she said next.

"Since the two of you are growing up, your father and I have decided to have more babies."

15

Sis spewed milk across the dining room. I decorated my new orange sweatshirt with goulash. Dad went into hysterics of joy. Being thirteen, I knew how babies were made, but my parents would not do that, would they?

Mom said, "We knew you would be surprised…"

Surprise was not the right word. *Terror!*

"…but now that you're older, we can be frank with you."

Uh-oh.

"Both you and I almost died when you were born, Corey, so I had surgery. I can't have babies anymore."

That was a relief. So, what was this baby thing about?

"We have decided to take in foster children."

Foster children? The only two I knew from Hanway Middle School—the Bosley twins—were *really* weird, which I guessed was because of the weird things that had happened to them.

Isn't my family weird enough without bringing in outside help?

"Our plan is to take little ones, under five years old, maybe even newborns. We'll need your cooperation."

My sister's eyes went blurry. I suspect she was thinking. I had never before had seen that. Her lips started moving without words as if she were practicing lines in a play before she heard her cue. When she was ready, she turned to Mom.

"Can I feed them and play with them and rock them to sleep and sing lullabies?"

Lullabies? Did she know any? Babies wouldn't go to sleep to hip hop, would they?

Mom replied, "Of course you can, honey. That would be wonderful."

"Can I give them baths?"

"Yes, I'll teach you how."

Babies were outside my experience, but I wasn't dumb enough to think they only ate and slept. I asked, "You won't make me change diapers, will you?"

"No, dear. We won't make you do that."

"Where will they sleep?" I asked. "We only have three bedrooms."

Mom tilted her head to the side. "That depends. The infants will sleep in the same room as Dad and me, but once they start walking and talking, the boys will stay in your room. Is that okay?"

Sis said, "I want a baby girl to sleep in my room."

"We'll see. We'll learn as we go, but we have to follow the rules. Your father and I will be going to foster parent training classes next week."

Questions pinged around in my brain like the pinball in the arcade. Someone might be living in my room, messing with my stuff? Would I have to clean my room? Babies cry in the middle of the night, right? I would need to buy earplugs. I didn't like this development, but I did like my newer, happier parents. God knows, with all the disasters happening in my life I could use one happy place to be.

When Mom turned to me for my answer, I thought of the power she and Dad were giving me to nix the plan. I couldn't do it. My family needed me. Imagine that. I said, "Okay."

Sis asked, "But Mom, who will take care of the baby when you're at work and I'm in school?"

Mom answered, "Foster care pays a little bit, so I'll quit my job at Belle's. We'll get by."

Crash! No money for spareribs or pot roasts? I do like mac-and-cheese, but not every night.

ooo

Mac-and-cheese at school is not the same. They use chopped spaghetti squash instead of macaroni, tofu curds instead of cheese, and plain low-fat yogurt instead of cream. Yet it was still better than most of their food. I smuggled in

17

some Cheez-It's to mix with it.

The Buds table was quiet, adjusting to our new reality. More people meant less trust. Sarah and Hu sat on one side of the table, Justine and Harley on the other side, me at one end. Jimmy decided to stay with the Studs, although if my sister ever darkened the door of the school cafeteria he would have sat at her feet.

I decided to break the silence with my news.

"My mom and dad have decided to be foster parents. We're going to have little kids in our house."

"Wow!" said Sarah.

"Bombshell," said Hu.

Justine said, "E-e-e-y-e-w!"

"Why are they doing that?" asked Harley.

"They miss having kids in the house now that I've grown up."

"As if," said Sarah.

Hu snorted. "Grown up? You?"

"E-e-e-y-e-w," added Justine.

Harley said, "That will change things"

"Sure will," I said. "I'll have little brothers and sisters. The boy kind will be in my room, except they'll sleep in Mom's room while they're babies."

Sarah had the same look as my sister when she said, "Babies are nice."

"Ick!" Justine said. "Babies poop."

"As if you don't," said Harley.

"What's it like to have a brother or sister?" Hu asked.

We all stared at him. We hadn't realized that he might feel left out by not having one.

Justine looked over at her brother. "They can be a real pain in the neck."

He responded, "But I guess you're stuck with loving them anyway."

"My big sister is my best friend," Sarah said. "We talk about things we wouldn't tell anybody else, certainly not our mom and dad."

I asked, "Not even us?"

"Not *ever* you."

I added my bit. "I can't figure my sister out. She can be really nice, and one minute later she can be extra snotty. Sometimes I like her, other times I don't, but I never understand her."

Hu got philosophical. "Does anyone ever understand anyone else?"

Justine changed the subject. "Aren't foster kids kind of wrecked? Like the Bosley twins? They are one hundred percent nutty."

People would scatter to the edges of the hallway as the Bosleys sauntered past side by side, dressed all in black, dyed black hair cut exactly the same with a white streak down the middle, faces blank. Tommy and Tori. They never talk, not to anybody. You could not tell them apart except when they entered the bathrooms. We think Tori's a girl, and Tommy's a boy. They should wear name tags.

Harley said, "Being foster kids really messed them up."

"It might not be that," Hu speculated. "The cause could be genetic. Maybe when they were inside their mother their brains got switched, and even they don't know who they are."

E-e-e-e-e-y-e-e-e-w!

We sat silent in awe of that vision for a while before Harley asked me, "So what happened when you were in the principal's office yesterday?"

"You know about that?"

"Everybody knows about that."

Yeesh. I would have to come clean, or at least semi-clean, like washing your face but not behind your ears.

Justine inquired, "Will they let foster kids in your house if you are a criminal?"

"I'm not a criminal. I was framed!"

"Everybody knows that, too," Harley said, "but no eyewitnesses will be coming forward."

"Yeah," wondered Sarah, "why didn't the police haul you off to Juvie like they did Amy last fall? Why haven't you been suspended from school?"

"Principal Farraday calls it possession, not distribution like Amy did. I'm on parole."

"That's all?"

"I'm off the track team this spring."

"Bummer."

"Not really. Coach Hardesty twisted my arm to run track, but I don't like the way he chews kids out when they make mistakes. He makes them feel like worms. I can feel wormy without his help."

"So that's it?" Hu said. "You got off easy?"

"That's it, unless you guys are going to throw me out of the Buds."

"We won't, but don't try going back to the Studs," Sarah cautioned.

"Don't worry. They won't want me anyway, since I've been kicked off the track team."

Sarah and Hu put out their hands over the fake-mac-and-cheese, I put my hands over theirs, Justine put her hands on mine, and Harley, for the first time, added his.

Buds forever, loyal and true!

4

007

I ran alone in Butterworth Park after school. Winter had attacked our cross country course, digging trenches, setting branch traps, leaving mud slicks, and reeking destruction like yesterday had done to my life. Both needed to be rebuilt.

My friends didn't know I was the principal's snitch. Sarah and Hu could be trusted, but I didn't want them to know. I'd never had much to hide before, except myself, and I felt guilty. But what choice did I have? If I defied Principal Farraday, I was done for. If I betrayed the Scuds, I would never have peace.

I liked Harley but didn't know how far I could trust him. I knew Justine, felt sorry for her and guilty that my discovering her secret life as the Prankster last fall had meant her mother wouldn't talk to her anymore, but, because of that, I didn't trust her very much. As for the foster children deal, I shuddered in fear that my house might be invaded by a preschool version of Tommy and Tori.

My future? All I could see was damp, dark fog.

However, as I loped up the driveway to my house, out of the fog shone a bright light—my father in all his orange glory.

"Change into your running clothes, Corey. Let's hit the pavement!"

"Do I have to change, Dad?"

"Of course you do. Everyone should know that we are father and son, one in spirit, two peas in a pod, two peanuts in one shell."

More like two pumpkins on one vine. But I did it, and we walk-jog-walk-jog-walked the same three blocks. Just in case Mom was watching, I think, we sprinted the last 30 feet out of the fog up the driveway. Then he bent over and panted before he said, "Guess what's on tonight?"

I knew that meant TV. My guess was, "WTA wrestling?"

"No. That's Mondays… (pant) Tonight's 007… (puff)… James Bond… (sigh) You're old enough now. Let's watch it together."

My father is into James Bond, big time. Maybe he was a spy in some past life. He scans the TV Guide and surfs the 237 channels we get on cable for any movie, any version. He had invited himself into my running world. Now he was inviting me into his world of espionage. Little did he know I was already a spy.

Supper that night was extraordinary. We each got our favorites. Mom made Dad liver and onions. Sis had chicken strips and cheesy mashed potatoes. I had pancakes and sausage. Mom had cream of broccoli soup plus a tomato and cucumber sandwich. Either Mom was cleaning out the refrigerator or she wanted us all in a good mood.

When we were full and happy, she said, "We have good

news and bad news."

Uh-oh. I had my fill of bad news, although good news would be welcome.

"The good news is that your father and I took the day off today and attended our first foster parenting class. We filled out the paperwork, and we seem to qualify. The first session was about the basic rules and laws we need to follow. We will need to baby-proof the house, which we will all do together on Saturday, since you need to understand how to keep it that way. My kitchen meets their code already, so that isn't a problem. I'll put baby locks on the cupboards and drawers. We can't get a dog or a cat, because of potential allergies.

Personally, I had never had a dog or wanted one. My experience with the neighbors' barking, growling, nipping-at-my-heels dogs was enough exposure for me.

"The bad news is that you can't share a room with them."

That sounded like good news to me.

"A-a-w-w," groaned my sister.

"Sorry. State law. But you can bathe, feed, and rock the babies, once you are trained in the correct way to do it."

Wait a minute.

I asked, "Mom, where can they sleep? Our house only has three bedrooms."

"Not exactly. We have the guest room in the basement."

So, the poor little kid would be sleeping in the basement with the mice. The good news was that no mouse could ever make it upstairs. My father had set thirty-seven mouse traps of six different varieties all around the basement and up the stairway. Mice came in from somewhere every day, but none made it out of the dungeon. Dad emptied traps before bed each night, restocking the bait in them. He used a pound of cheese a week. We would have to keep Band-Aids in stock, too, for foster kids' toes.

"Corey, we're going to move you into the guest room."

Next up, Dad and I watched Bond, James Bond, through two long movies. If I lived in 007's world, I would know what to do. He always knew what to do.

During the night I had a dream that I was a double agent, with his cover blown, being shot at from both sides. I looked down and found myself full of holes like Swiss cheese, and hundreds of mice were nibbling me to death.

The good news was that I woke up with an idea. Maybe, just maybe, I could play both Principal Farraday's game and the Scud's game, too, and they would dual each other to a stalemate. I could come out the winner at school anyway. A dream's a dream, after all.

ooo

Once again, the next day, I felt the ham-hand of the law. Principal Farraday demanded, "What profit do you postulate to procure from your perspicuity?"

I think he wanted a report. "They sell candy bars in the hallway before lunch."

"And what personages perpetrate this peccadillo?"

That meant who-done-it. "I can't say yet, but I'll keep watching."

That was not exactly a lie, although it felt like one. I couldn't say what he wanted to hear if I knew what was good for me.

"Perfect," he declared, pushing me back into the hallway. Now I really had to watch my steps. I counted 27 before I felt another fat hand, and I was propelled—I mean yanked— through another door. Noford held me captive in the boy's room.

"Whaterya doin' with the principal in his office, and why ain'tya suspended?"

Just then another kid came through the doorway, holding himself and bouncing up and down. He saw Noford and plunged back out again. I hoped he made it to the other boy's room in time. Out of his backpack Booger pulled a hand-lettered sign and a roll of tape. He slapped the sign on the outside of the door and closed it. The sign said, "OUT OF ODER."

"Give," growled Noford.

I gave him my lunch money.

He took it and said, "No, I mean give it up, what'er you an' Farraday up to?"

"He put me on parole for possession. I have to report in every so often."

"Sounds right. Parole. My Pop has to do that, too. So, here's the deal. You report to the blue, you report to me, too. Haw! How's that, Booger? I made a poim!"

"A poim, a poim. Haw."

Noford hunched down to my face, bad breath and all, and hissed, "He's after us, ain't he. What's he know?"

"He knows that somebody is selling candy in the hallway before lunch. He doesn't know it's you. You'll need to stop doing that before he catches you."

"Okay. Good. Ain't so bad to tell the truth, huh?" He gave me back my lunch money. "Now you's one of us, undercover, like. How's that feel?"

It felt slimy. Now I was a Bud, and a Scud, and a Snitch, all at the same time. How could I keep them all separate with no one the wiser?

At least I was no longer a Stud.

My legs felt numb as I staggered down the hall to the cafeteria and over to the Buds' table.

"What's wrong with you?" Hu asked shaking his head.

"Tough night, not much sleep, James Bond movies, spies, double agents in my house, foster kids in my room. I'm going into exile like Napoleon on the island of Elba, being nibbled to death by mice in the boy's room, perpetrating a peccadillo."

Sarah frowned. "You aren't making sense, Corey."

Hu grabbed a jumbo sprig of parsley from his goat-cheese-and-greens salad and whipped it back and forth across my face. "Snap out of it!"

That's what I needed, I guess. I took a deep breath, sat down and held my head in my hands. "Sorry, I am having a really bad week, really bad. I don't know what to do."

Sarah said, "Yeah, we get it. You got caught by Farraday. You're getting foster kids in your house. You have a lot to adjust to, Corey."

"You don't know the half of it," I groaned.

She smiled. "What you need is a distraction. We have just the thing you need. Do you want to spend a day with us over Easter Break?"

Our school system may be the last one in the country which still takes an Easter Break at Easter, rather than a Spring Break at some other time. Easter was a week from Sunday, so we would be out of school all next week.

She continued, "Our church believes in youth service projects, so next Tuesday our JV Youth Group will be cleaning up yards for old people. All the other Buds are signed up already. Do you want to join us?"

"Okay."

"Good. Pastor Rusk says that the best way to get your mind off your own troubles is to help other people with theirs."

I could use a little brainless work. Maybe if I wasn't looking for it my brain would return. Leave it alone and it'll come home. Never mind.

Also, I wanted to see Coach Rusk again.

5

EASTER BREAK

aby-proofing a house is hard. I guess babies can't tell what stuff is food so they eat everything. They also like to stick things in places where they don't belong, like pencils in their eyes and forks in electrical outlets. All small things they could swallow and sharp things they could poke into other things have to be put up high or locked away.

They like to open drawers so they can climb on them to throw themselves off them to find out if it hurts. They jump off tables, desks, and sofas to see if they can fly. I can't believe babies are so dumb.

Mom says, "Yes, they are, and so were you."

Our family spent the first Saturday of Easter Break examining every item and every inch until everything was shelved up high, boxed or closeted, hidden, locked, padded, screwed to the wall, plugged and sanitized. Sis had to do her own room, and she loved doing it. She asked Mom, "Can we borrow somebody's two-year-old to try it out?"

Mom answered, "That will come soon enough, after we pass inspection by a social worker next week."

I saw two good things about that day. The first was that I did not need to baby-proof my stuff because I could continue to live upstairs until a kid needed my room. When I moved downstairs the hazards would go with me. The second good thing was that, since Mom couldn't cook that day, Dad and I went to Pepperoni Pete's Pizza Place for carry-out. Pete's special, my favorite, is hamburger pizza with M & M's and toasted marshmallows.

Oh, one other thing. Dad had me stand at the door to the basement and reach as high as I could, which is where he put a slide bolt that worked from both sides. That way no kid smaller than me could experience mouse-trap-snap.

000

Easter Good Deeds Day fell on Monday. I ran to the church. All the Buds were there and none of the Scuds, which made it a good place to be. Since Ferdy, Jimmy and Cherise were there, I knew half of the sixteen kids. If Sis had known Jimmy was there, she would have come with me. Mr. Highcourt, Harley and Justine's father brought them. Ferdy's mom was there, too, tall, thin, tired, and sad. I knew she worked long days running Hanway's only laundromat for the owner, who only came to help when Ferdy's mom needed a break. I recognized her from last winter when our washer broke down, and from the conference cross country meet last fall.

Coach Rusk—Pastor Rusk—gathered us all around him.

"Thank you for giving your day to people who need your help. God will reward you, but your best compensation will be how good this makes you feel. We have nine projects. We will divide into three teams, each with three places to go. Mr. Highcourt will lead team one, Mrs. Phillips will take team two, and team three is mine!" He rung his hands and cackled. "All

29

mine, heh, heh, heh, heh!"

Coach divided the kids three ways, gave assignments and instructions, led us all in prayer, and sent off team one in the Highcourts' new Town and Country van. Team two used Ferdy's beat up Astro. My team was Coach Rusk, Sarah, Hu, and me, plus two kids I didn't know. We piled into the church van, with rakes, shovels, hedge shears, loppers, and more.

I didn't know the Miller's, but I knew their house by running past it. A scraggly terrier behind their chain-link fence wanted desperately to chew off my leg. We waited on the sidewalk outside the fence with our gear. The dog averaged three barks a second according to my watch.

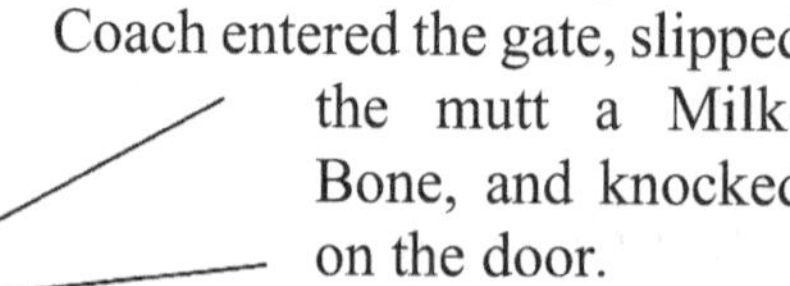

Coach entered the gate, slipped the mutt a Milk-Bone, and knocked on the door.

Mrs. Miller opened up, smiled at Coach, and yelled, "King, house!"

The dog scrambled inside. Then Mr. Miller wheeled his chair unto the porch, talked with Coach, pointed at two small trees, plus the fence, swept his arm over the whole yard, and rolled back inside. Once the door closed, we hauled in the tools, lined them up inside the fence, and fanned through the yard picking up sticks and trash and debris. Then we split up.

My assignment was to clean up King's pen, a disgusting fenced-in square in the back yard. I gathered a full bucket of chewed up dog toys and a trash bag of dog poop.

Sarah and the two others trimmed hedges, Hu pulled up the dead grass and weeds caught in the fence from last fall, and Coach Rusk pruned the dwarf apple trees and gave the lawn its first mowing of the year.

When we were loading the van, the Millers came to the porch and waved. I think they were saying thank you, but King raced to the fence and machine-gunned us with barks. Coach tossed him another bone, and Sarah blew him a kiss.

Our second job was uneventful yard clean up, cutting and trimming grass, but it ended nicely. Mrs. Sweeny invited us inside for milk and homemade oatmeal cookies, two each. Then, at noon, all three groups met at church for sloppy joes, chips, and ice cream. We shared our morning experiences. Coach prayed for the people we had helped.

Our afternoon assignment was something different. Professor Peavy looked, like, ninety-five, with his face one big wrinkle hanging down like a basset hound. He wanted everything done right, or you would hear about it. When we washed windows, he stood inside pointing to the spots we missed. While we washed his 1977 Olds Omega, he rummaged in the garage for a dried can of Turtle Wax, which made putting the wax on like rubbing a car with a bar of soap. He complained that some spots didn't shine.

I said, "That's rust, Sir. It doesn't shine."

He grumbled. "Nonsense. Do it again."

Coach had the others do the yard clean up, while he and I weeded the rose garden in front of the house. He'd brought an old flannel shirt for me to wear, and leather gloves, both too big for me, but I was glad to have them. The thorns were brutal. This was our chance to talk.

"Corey, Coach Hardesty said you left the track team."

"Not exactly."

"Then what, exactly? I know you love to run, and you respond well to pressure, so why would you quit the team?"

At that point I had to make a decision. How much could I trust Coach Rusk? I really needed somebody to listen to me, and he was the only adult I had ever known who listened.

"I didn't quit, Coach. I was kicked off."

"Why, Corey? You aren't a troublemaker."

"No, I don't make trouble, but I collect it."

"Coach Hardesty just told me that the principal informed him that you would no longer be on the team."

"Yeah, that's true." (Ouch! The thorns.)

"So, what did you do wrong?"

"Nothing. It's what was done to me." Then the dam broke, everything poured out, the whole mess—the Twix, the principal, the snitch thing, the Scuds, the neon orange sweat suit, the foster kids, the basement, the mice—everything.

"Wow!" Pastor Rusk exclaimed. "You really had a bad week."

"What should I do, Coach?"

"Corey, I won't tell you what to do. Part of growing into a man is wrestling with right and wrong, and choosing the right way."

"But I don't see any right way. Everything seems wrong."

"There is a right way. You just need to find it. The right way is not usually the easy way, but you can feel good about it afterward, and that makes you feel good about yourself."

"Don't you have any help for me?"

"Well, I live my life by principles. Your principles could be different. A couple of mine come to mind. First, *love both your friends and your enemies,* and second, *be who you are, not who someone else wants you to be.*"

A gruff voice behind us yelled, "Aren't you done yet? What's taking so long? I need my peace and quiet." Then he slammed the door.

"That man is mean!" I said.

"Not really, Corey. He's just old and disappointed with his life. That happens when you only live for yourself. What he really needs is love."

Our talk made me feel both better and worse.

Better because Coach heard my story and didn't judge me, but worse because I might have to love the Scuds.

What good could possibly come out of this mess?

6

CHANGES

I felt better for the rest of that week at least. With no principal, no Scuds, no homework, plus a good deed done, I felt free. The weather was nice. Hu didn't need to work at the Peking Pagoda until three-thirty, so we spent the days together running in Butterworth, climbing trees and playing Frisbee. I could throw a Frisbee straight. Hu could make it curve either way with either hand, hang in the air like a helicopter or come back to him like a boomerang.

"How do you do that?" I asked.

"Physics," he answered.

On Thursday, Hu said, "You seem more like your old self."

"Thanks, I think."

"I'm serious. You've been so tight lately, like when you blow a balloon so full of air that it might explode."

I said, "I'm sorry."

He said, "I'm your friend. You can talk to me."

34

I replied, "I know that."

What I thought was, *You are my first BFF, and if I tell you what I told Coach Rusk, you could be in as much trouble at Hanway school as I am.*

ꞷꞷꞷ

Why do they call Good Friday good, since that's the day Jesus was killed? The humpback preacher told the story so well that it made me mad. I felt like that Simon who was forced to carry that cross up that Via Dolorosa Street place, which made him feel like an accomplice to Jesus' murder. At least they didn't hang Simon on it.

I like history, and the preacher said the story was in the Bible. I found ours in the bottom drawer of Mom's china cabinet under the cloth napkins. It took me a while to find the place, but I read it out loud to myself in my room. Why do they do those things to innocent people? Why do they twist it around to call it good? Why do kids need foster homes, anyway?

Dad gets Good Friday off work at the mattress factory, but I guess our state doesn't consider it a holiday, since that was the day Mr. Fink, the social worker, decided to invade our house. Mom took the morning off so she could be on display with the rest of us, inspected like a new shipment of orangutans at a zoo.

First, Mr. Fink talked to each of us separately, asking stupid questions like, "Do you feel safe at home?" I said yes but thought *until you walked in.* He asked, "If your father was an animal, what would he be?" I said, "a horse," but I don't know why. The man recorded every word, for evidence of something, I suppose. At least he didn't make me sign it.

Then he inspected the house room by room—living room, dining room, kitchen, my parents' room and my sister's—and found them all perfect. Then he asked, "Where will your foster

35

child sleep?"

Mom replied, "We asked for babies. We will put a crib in our bedroom."

Mr. Fink stated, "That is acceptable. However, when the child outgrows the crib ..."

"Well, we haven't yet ..."

"Just the facts, Ma'am."

"Well, it will be Corey's room, but ..."

"Show me your room, boy."

I shuffled over to my door, which Mom had left closed, and opened it. Mr. Fink went in. Mr. Fink backed out.

"Holy— (he used an unacceptable word, so I will supply another one) —cow!"

He slammed the door. "You fail for now. I will return a week from today. Have that room safe, clean, and thoroughly, I mean *completely,* sanitized."

The rest of my Easter Break was spent walking my own Via Dolorosa, from my room to the basement, moving thirteen years of my life. When my arms were loaded, I couldn't see where I stepped, so I got snapped by every mousetrap on the stairway. I couldn't run for three days.

My Mom sorted all my things, threw out the good stuff, and arranged the junk neatly in my cell. She said, "Keep it this way until next Friday!"

On Thursday evening, Dad hid all weapons of mouse destruction in the garage. He pried open the basement door to the outside that we never used, oiled the hinges, and installed a spring lock, so I could get out in an emergency. On Friday, Mr. Fink returned. My old room was perfectly empty except for a bed and dresser. He demanded to see the basement, since "the accommodations must be up to code for all the household residents." We held our breath hoping no mice decided to join the party, but I guess they were as scared of Mr. Fink as we were. We passed.

For a smart man, Principal Farraday can be surprisingly un-smart. He stood in the hallway before lunch with a clipboard under his arm and an iPhone in his hand. He pretended to be texting or checking e-mail, but everybody knew the truth. He was taking pictures.

What he got was a nice album full of students smiling and waving. The teacher who was the cafeteria monitor that day was getting the same result with her phone at the other end of the hallway, which left the lunchroom wide open for business. The Scuds had their best sales day yet, and the cafeteria ladies didn't mind, since they got free candy.

I informed the principal after lunch that his enemies had moved into the dining hall, and told the Scuds, so the next day Mr. Farraday and the monitor were "texting" there, while the Scuds were back selling candy in the hallway. Lunch was a seaweed dog in a gluten-free bun. The Scuds' customers pulled the candy out of the wrappers, pocketed them, bought lunch, trashed the seaweed, and enjoyed chocolate dogs.

Back and forth it went for days. By May, a new system was in place. Someone else must have been masterminding this besides Noford. People would slip a dollar to Booger who greeted them with a handshake at the door. Inside the door they would shake Noford's hand, he would sniff it, and if it smelled Booger-ish he would give them a sticker, maybe Scooby-doo or Dora or Spidey, a different one each day.

Of course, they would go back the bathroom to wash their Booger-hands, at which time they would peal the sticker off the backing, wear it, read the backing, and go to the number of the empty locker that held the candy that day. In the crowd around the locker, all wearing stickers, was a confederate, no one knew who, but I think it was Amy, the girl who had run the locker candy store last fall.

If anyone took more than one candy bar, or didn't have

the right sticker, the next day Booger would greet them with a nice warm, smelly hug.

That stopped the cheating.

All Principal Farraday said was, "What pleasant people, promoting school spirit, plus providing pictography, though I do pity the one that produces such a putrefactive presence."

7

GRADUATION

Nothing much new happened for the rest of the school year. The Scuds played hide-and-seek with the principal, while I played dodge ball with both sides, trying not to be anyone's target. My Buds adjusted to being a group of five, although Justine's pouty presence formed a small cloud, and Harley's "Adonis" looks drew Sarah's stares. My family negotiated the DCFS maze, while I searched sales flyers for steel-tipped shoes in my size.

Sarah and Hu invited me to a church Youth Group meeting on a Sunday in May. Though compared to the Pumpkin Party last fall this one was tame, I was glad to see Coach. When he asked, "how are you," I knew he meant it, and when I said, "okay so far," I knew he understood. He told the group about a week of summer camp he was leading on Lake Havacrappie, with swimming, canoeing, volleyball, campfires, and the camp cook's specialty, pickle loaf.

After the meeting, Coach Rusk asked me, "Do you want to go?"

"Sounds great, but I don't think my dad can afford it."

Hu said, "It's free to you. We raised money all year for

camp, and we have enough for all the youth group and five friends. We nominated you."

Wow. Nobody ever did anything so nice for me before. I wondered if Harley and Justine were going, but Coach said they would be vacationing in Colorado. Wow. The original three Buds could be together for a whole week.

"I'll have to ask my parents."

The next night over homemade *chow mein* with those crunchy noodles, I brought up the subject.

"Dad, can I go to camp?"

Sis asked, "Boot camp?"

"No. Summer camp."

"All summer, I hope, I hope."

"No. One week."

"Where?" Mom asked.

"Camp Carmel."

Dad wondered, out loud, "Why would they name a camp after candy?"

"Not caramel. Carmel." This conversation was not starting well, so I thought I'd better take more control. "Hu and Sarah's youth group is going to camp in July at Camp Carmel on Lake Havacrappie, and they've invited me to come with them. Can I go?"

"We can't afford it."

"It's free."

"Sounds too cheap. Do they feed you? Do you sleep on the ground? Do they have running water and bathrooms?"

"No, no and yes. It's quite nice. I saw pictures."

"Tents or teepees?"

"They have cabins with bunk beds, bathrooms with showers, a swimming pool with lifeguards, and a dining hall with a real cook who makes pickle loaf."

"Ugh," contributed my sister.

"Can I go?"

"Are there adults?"

"Yes, adult counselors, and Coach Rusk is in charge. Can I go?"

"Okay," said Dad.

"Okay," said Mom.

"Please do," said Sis.

ooo

Our first foster baby came the week before Sis's Eighth Grade Graduation. Yes, our school still does that. The baby's name was Aloysius, three months old, only nine pounds, and up for adoption. All he did was cry—all day, all night, when you rocked him, even when he ate—possibly because he was named Aloysius. Only the mice and I in the basement got any sleep.

By Sunday's graduation day, Mom, Dad and Sis were zombies. My sister did her makeup with her eyes closed, so she looked like the walking dead.

Dad put a tie on over his t-shirt, drank a pot of coffee, and drove. Sis sat in front with her head against the window, which made one side of her hair flat. In the back, in the middle of his space capsule car seat, little A-lo kicked his feet and cursed in baby language.

Mom stuck a baby bottle in his ear. Being the only remaining human in the car, I fastened every person's seatbelt and climbed in beside the baby, who stopped bawling with a gulp, and ogled me.

The quiet was so sudden they all woke up.

"He likes Corey!" Sis exclaimed. "Can you believe it? Corey has a new friend!"

Dad opened his eyes and drove, Mom opened hers and moved the bottle to the baby's mouth, and Sis opened both eyes at once and stopped leaking brain tissue.

41

A-lo and I had a staring contest. He won. I was elected by my family, 3-1, to be the baby holder, in the corner of the school auditorium, by the back door. Sis trudged into the robe-ing room for her zombie duds.

Mom and Dad sat in the second-row front with their Polaroid camera (an old-timey contraption that spits out a plastic photo as soon as you click the 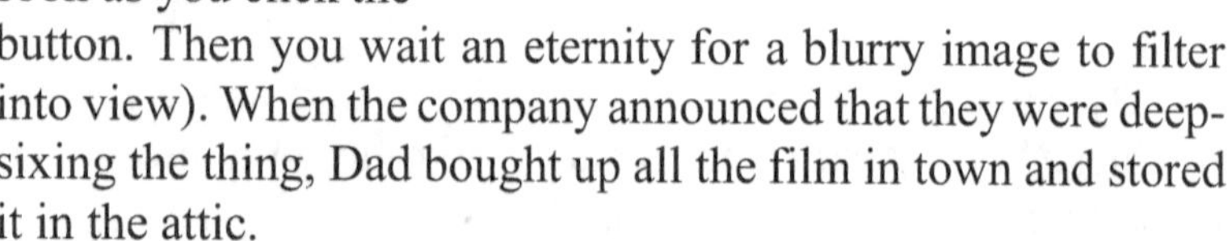 button. Then you wait an eternity for a blurry image to filter into view). When the company announced that they were deep-sixing the thing, Dad bought up all the film in town and stored it in the attic.

Dad put his arm around Mom, leaned in cheek-to-cheek, and stayed that way. From the back it looked romantic, but I knew what they really were doing.

When the middle school band struck up *Pomp and Circumstance* without the eighth-grade musicians, it sounded more like *Bombs and Accidents.* That woke up even my parents, but not the baby, who just farted and pooped his pants. People coming in late would start to slide past me into the back row, smile at him, sniff, and back away fast.

The procession was long and slow. All the graduates were shivering. I spotted Cherise first, rocking with the rhythm of some other music, because she had ear buds. A while later Harley was solemn and poised, as if this was an important occasion. Jimmy came along about three minutes after that, eyes darting around like a running back searching for a seam to dash through for daylight. The very last graduate in the line was my sister, sixteen steps behind the others, dragging along like a wounded soldier on the last day of a brutal war.

The program began with a flute and piccolo duet called *Larghetto*, which actually sounded like two small birds fighting over a worm. Then Principal Farraday gave a speech featuring the letter "Q." Who knew there could be so many "Q" words besides "quiet"? The adults seemed to understand it better than I did, and they found it quite amusing.

Being a Zilch has its consequences. Sis, as the last one in the alphabet, sat at the end of the front row next to a post holding the ragged, heavy stage curtain. During the principal's speech about "Quintessential Quaint Quotations," while all the other graduates wrapped their arms around themselves with their teeth chattering, Sis wrapped the stage curtain around her, leaned against the post and slept. Only her face showed, with a grimace, like a creature from the living dead waiting to devour the brains of the graduates, since it had none of its own.

At last, what we had been waiting for, the diplomas. Well, they weren't really diplomas. They were a Certificate of Accomplishment, in a used pocket folder, because of school budget cuts. But the graduates were thrilled to have them and shake Principal Farraday's hand. They could say goodbye to him forever.

Each graduate's name was announced, last name first, along with any honors he or she had received. Cherise, our best girl cross country runner, got Musician of the Year. Harley was honored as Student Council President. Jimmy was Athlete of the Year. At every name the crowd clapped, whether the person got an award or not.

When they finally got to my sister she was still snuggled in the curtain. Principal Farraday announced "Zilch." Nothing. "Zilch." Nothing. He leaned into the microphone and yelled, "Zilch, Cheerleader of the Year!" Sis jumped up, stumbled out, staggered over, knocked a chair down, grabbed her certificate and ran back behind the curtain.

This time the audience stood, clapped and cheered. They thought it was an act, and she was extraordinarily clever.

They call those funny hats they wear mortarboards. A mortar is either a weapon of war or cement that goes between bricks. The graduates threw their mortars in the air. It was a wonder no one got injured.

When it was over, my parents retrieved Sis and dragged her into the lobby.

Sis mumbled, "We have to move to Poland."

But she was the most popular person there. How come things go that way for her?

Cherise gave her a high five, saying, "You go, girl!" and "Great makeup, too."

Harley grinned. "That was awesome."

Jimmy sidled up and whispered, "Hi, sleeping beauty. Can I wake you up with a kiss?"

She kept her zombie face. They all assumed she was staying in character, playing the part to the last line, preparing for stardom in Hollywood. She actually *was* the walking dead.

No one surrounded me. Mom took A-lo away to change him but left the aroma with me. She brought him back screaming, handed him to me, and he stopped crying and stared. Maybe he recognized me as a fellow reject from life.

When we got home, Mom sat A-lo and me in the rocking chair, handed me a bottle, turned on a 24-hour *Gilligan's Island* marathon, and they all went to bed. I watched and rocked. He ate and slept. It wasn't at all that bad. *(Another old show you should check out, I mean, what a nutty bunch to be stranded with!)*

After a while, Sis came out of her room, sat on the sofa and said, "Thank you for trying to help."

There is a first time for everything.

She said, "We have to move to Norway."
I said, "Norway is cold."
"Not as cold as tonight was."
I asked, "Why was everyone shivering up there, anyway? I wasn't cold."
"The robes. The cafeteria ladies forgot to take them out of the meat locker ahead of time."
"Why were they in the meat locker?"
"Well, since the school hardly ever serves meat any more that's where they store the graduation robes."
"Are you okay?"
"I am really, really embarrassed."
"Why? People loved you. How do you do that?"
"I don't know. I was just being who I am."
"I'm just myself, and people don't love me."
"Your friends do."
"They do?"
"Sarah does."
"Really?"
"Yeah. You aren't as bad as you think."
"You aren't as bad as I thought either."
"Thanks."
"Thanks."
She went back to bed.
I went back to Gilligan.
Maybe in the morning both A-lo and I could get our baths.

☿

CAMP CARMEL

A-lo and I had three great days together. I even learned how to change his diapers and heat up his bottle. But mostly he and Mom and Sis slept while I rocked away and watched reruns of *Monk* on TV—wondering if I'd turn out like him—and read biographies of Patrick Henry, Gandhi, and Roger Bannister that had somehow found their way into our bookcase. (If you've never seen *Monk,* you should. He's worried about *everything, all the time,* which is precisely what makes him an excellent detective!)

Then DCFS came to get my little brother.

Someone wanted to adopt him. I had asked Mom and Dad if we could, and they said "NO!" I guess it's just as well. I couldn't have taken A-lo to camp with me.

We gathered at Grace Baptist Church on Sunday afternoon. Hu and I had each packed all our stuff in a sports bag. Sarah had two suitcases. Ferdy and Cherise were going, too, along with a bunch of other kids I didn't know.

Pastor drove us in the church bus to the only pretty corner of our state where they had dammed up a small river to make Lake Havacrappie, which was named after a fish by a contest of third graders, but not pronounced the same as the fish. Camp Carmel is on a slope looking across the water toward the sunrise.

I learned two things right away about summer camp. First, you can't lie around in your PJs in the morning and eat potato chips, like at home. You have a schedule, and you had better follow it. You eat whatever is available to eat, including pickle loaf, or you don't eat at all.

Second, you have to clean your room, which is a cabin with eight kids and a counselor, and you have to pass inspection, or you get demerits. You sleep in bunk beds which you have to make so tight that a dime would bounce on it. Hu could do it. I couldn't. If it weren't for Hu, I would have earned a demerit every day. Ten demerits meant your cabin got kitchen duty, or bathroom duty, or worst of all, you had to sing nursery rhymes for everybody at breakfast.

At six in the morning, our counselor, a muscled college student named Juan, stepped outside, threw open the shutters, and yelled, "Rise and shine, campers! Behold the glory of God!"

I was fast asleep on the top bunk in front of the window in my undershorts because of the heat. The sun blazed over the lake, and doubled its effect by reflecting in the water, and both lights shown directly through my window. I was in the spotlight, in my tidy whities, for all the world to see.

I scrambled on my belly toward the ladder at the same time as a startled Ferdy on the bunk below knocked the ladder on the floor. My feet landed, not on the ladder, but on Ferdy. With nothing to stop me I slid securely onto his shoulders.

He said, "Not now, Zip. That's a pool game."

Juan said, "Who's Zip? I thought your name was Corey."
Ferdy said, "We call him Zip because he runs fast."
"Good to know. You can be our anchor leg in the relay races. From now on, I dub you Sir Zipparoo!" He tapped me with a fly swatter. "We shall be the Knights of Cabin 7. Ferdy, you are Sir Ferdinand. Hu, you are 'Hulyn the Magician.'"

Juan named all eight of us. For the whole week we galloped everywhere and called every girl "my Lady." They loved it. We also won every relay race that involved running. Have I told you that Hulyn can run fast, too?

The games were great, and the swimming was great. The first time I saw Sarah in a one-piece bathing suit was *Wow!* She gave me feelings I never had before.

The second night, as we gathered after dark at the campfire, Coach Rusk asked, "How many of you have ever been on a snipe hunt?" About three-quarters of them raised their hands with a grin. I thought, *that must mean fun.*

Juan said, "Can anyone tell the others what a snipe is?"

The lispy kid from Hanway, Leonard (whom Juan had knighted Sir Lean-hard) answered, "Ith a bird. Thomething like a little chicken that flyth in the dark."

"Yes, that's it. You never see them in daylight because they are night creatures that eat mosquitoes and lightening bugs. They run fast and fly close to the ground.”

“Yeah,” Cherise added, “they peck at your toes, so you’d better ditch your flip-flops for regular shoes.”

Those who had been on a snipe hunt before said things like—

“They taste good fried in butter.”

“Tomorrow is pickle loaf day, so if we want something good to eat for supper, we’d better catch some snipe tonight.”

“They have sharp beaks. You can’t catch snipe in paper bags, and plastic bags would smother them, so they wouldn’t be fresh for cooking. We have to use burlap sacks to keep them alive.”

“Those campers that don’t catch one have to kill and clean all the snipes for those that do, so you’d better catch one.”

“They’re small, like a one-person chicken, so it’s pickle loaf if you don’t catch one.”

“You spot them with flashlights. If you yell, ‘Snipe! Snipe!’ they get confused and take off and you can catch them in your open bag.”

Coach commanded, “Go spray yourselves with bug spray, put on shoes and jackets, and be back in five minutes.”

I made it back in three.

Some of the girls took seven.

Burlap sacks and flashlights were handed out before the counselors led us into the woods. When we got close to the lake, on cue from Coach, I mean Pastor, Rusk we all screamed "Snipe! Snipe! Snipe!"

Everything went crazy. Lights pointed in all directions, I could see things moving, but couldn't tell what they were, except for the backside of a raccoon running fast. A counselor yelled, "Over here!" All the flashlights shone on one patch of underbrush, and half the group lunged at it with open bags.

"I got one!"

"Me, too!"

That was Sarah's voice. I ran over to her. "Show it to me," I begged.

"No. If I open the bag, it will fly out. Catch your own."

Juan had one, too. I asked to see it. He said, "No. I hate pickle loaf."

By then, the flashlights were on another spot, so I scrambled over, bag open. Nothing.

"Okay," decided Pastor Rusk. "You need to get these back to camp before they peck their way through the bags. If you have one, follow Juan."

Coach stayed with those of us with empty sacks.

Experience must be the best teacher, because those who caught a snipe seemed to be the ones who had done this before.

After they left, Pastor gave us more instructions.

"Turn off the flashlights and be very still so the snipe who escaped will think it's safe to come back. They aren't very smart, you know. Stay very close together, count to 500 slowly in a whisper. Snipe don't hear very well. If you should hear some rustling sounds in the bushes, it will be the birds returning."

We did that. When we reached 500, we flashed our lights all around, screeching, "Snipe! Snipe! Here snipe!"

Nothing.

We charged into the bushes.

Nothing.

"I don't see any," one girl whimpered.

"I still haven't seen one," I groaned.

"I hate pickle loaf, and I don't even know what it is," another boy complained.

"Pastor Rusk," a girl asked, "where did all the snipes go?"

Nothing.

That's when it dawned on us that we had all been sniped.

When we got back to the campfire everybody there was laughing at us. We joined in. The best April Fools' joke of my life happened in July.

Oh, and, by the way, pickle loaf, it turned out, was just meatloaf served with a dill pickle. It was pretty good.

ₒₒₒ

Camp was fun, but sometimes serious, too. Every day ended with a campfire, songs, and one or two stories. Juan told us about a boy named David who brought down a giant bully with just a slingshot and a stone. A girls' counselor talked about this woman who hid spies under a pile of grass drying on her roof. Another night we learned about this kid named Sam who heard God's voice telling him what to do with his life. He did it, and it turned out good, and exciting, too. I wished God would do that for me. Hearing God's voice would help me when things were a mess.

We heard about Jesus' mother who was just a teenager who saw an angel, obeyed God, and has been admired ever since. Everybody knows her name, Mary. Another woman named Sarah had to wait until she was, like, ninety to have a baby. But God gave her one. I wondered if my Sarah wanted a baby someday. I hoped I wouldn't be a hundred before I had a little A-lo of my own.

Coach told us about Jesus Himself, who was only twelve when He camped out for three days in His church. He proved He could teach the teachers a thing or two! That reminded me of my friend Hu, the smartest person I know, who was teaching me new things all the time.

I think I learned more about the Bible in that one week than I had ever learned from the humpbacked preacher from Texas.

Thursday was Talent Night, which was funny even when it was not meant to be. People tried to juggle, cabins did silly skits, girls did bad ballet and good cartwheels, and boys told dumb knock-knock jokes.

But then there was Cherise? Wow!

She played guitar and sang a song about a girl who went to heaven. You felt like you could see the angels she described, and you were eating at a wedding feast, and you were singing with a choir of millions. Everybody asked for more, so she sang about flying with eagles and being baptized in the Jordan River.

Pastor Rusk thanked her, and told us, "Cherise wrote all these songs herself."

Yeesh. I wondered if I could ever do anything that important.

Friday was our last campfire. We toasted marshmallows, sang the songs we learned that week, and some kids talked about special things Jesus did for them. Coach asked us to each take a stick, toss it in the fire and share one thing we wanted the others to pray about.

Praying was not a usual thing for me. I pray in emergencies. Doesn't everybody? But to just talk to God like you were friends seemed kind of like wasting His time when He had bigger things to do. But the counselors said God wanted us to talk to Him that way.

Cherise asked for prayer that her songs could be used to "bless hearts."

Sarah asked prayer for her parents to get along better with each other.

Hu asked that his parents' restaurant would be successful.

Ferdy put two sticks in the fire because, "One of these is for my father who would agree with me, if he could be here. Since my dad was killed in Iraq, my mom has been so sad and lonely. Please pray for her to be happy again."

When it came to my turn, I asked Coach—Pastor—if I had to tell what it was about. I was thinking about my being a snitch, stuck between the principal and the Scuds and how guilty I felt keeping it all secret. Pastor Rusk looked into my eyes and said, "It's okay, Corey. God knows. Just call it an unspoken prayer."

As I sat back down between Sarah and Hu, Sarah took my hand. *Sarah held my hand!* She didn't let go, even after campfire was over. I walked with her back to her cabin. Stopping in front, Sarah said, "That was nice."

I lifted her hand up with mine. "This is nice."

"Yes," she said, and let go. "But that's all, Corey. We can't be boyfriend and girlfriend."

"Why not?"

"Because we need to stay friends. Boyfriends and girlfriends break up, and then they can't be friends anymore. I want us always to be friends."

I wanted that, too, so I let go of her hand.

PART II: WATERGATE

Skip this if you want to, but you'll miss something if you do.

Richard Nixon had his Watergate; I had my first day of eighth grade.

Summer was slow and easy, except for camp week, which gave me time for hanging with Hu and for going to the city library to find history books. One of them was about Watergate.

President Nixon had done some good stuff, but he was what Hu would call "paranoid."

I felt ashamed that I felt a little bad for him. He just wanted to win. He had won once, but once was not enough. So, he sent his gang to go break into this place called Watergate to find out the Democrat secrets. He had his own secrets, but he thought, to win, he had to know theirs.

Watergate was like a bad prank, but a serious problem when his guys got caught. If he'd just said, "my bad," he might have gotten away with it (probably not), but he lied about it.

The more he lied, blamed other people, claimed, "I'm not

a crook," the worse it got. He won the election, but lost all respect he ever had, and the White House, too.

I felt bad for him, because I knew the feeling. I was hoping the first day of eighth grade was my "do over."

Little did I know…

$$9$$

EIGHTH GRADE

Justine showed up at the first cross country practice on August 1. Harley and Cherise had graduated, but Ferdy, Betty Jean, and Tyler were back, plus three who were sixth graders last year—a boy and two girls. I figured that line-up made me "top gun."

Coach Rusk sent us all through the Butterworth Park trail to warm up. I ran next to Justine and this year she didn't shove me away. I said, brilliantly, "Hey, Justine."

"Hey, yourself."

"Are you joining the team this year?"

"I'm here, aren't I?"

"Why?"

"Because I like to run, and I want to show you that I'm better at it than you are."

"No way."

"Way, and I'll prove it. I've been practicing."

She stepped up the pace. I stayed with her. She went faster yet. I kept up, but it was hard. When we could see the finish line, she went into her kick. I had been running all summer with Hu, with my orange dad, and by myself, but I had not worked on my game. My kick was gone.

Yeesh, Justine was good. My reign as top gun had lasted about fifteen minutes.

"Most of you have gotten lazy," Coach Rusk scolded. "School starts in two weeks, and you will be in shape by then. Practice until then will be here at nine every morning except for Sunday, so you can relearn your fundamentals, recover your form, and strengthen your legs and lungs. Come ready to work your tails off."

My tail was off already, but I knew he was right. As the others left, Coach motioned me to come over.

"She beat you, didn't she."

"Yeah, she did."

"Why?"

"I got lazy."

"No. I know you, and you're not lazy. You got complacent."

"What does that mean?"

"You got satisfied with yourself, thinking because you won the cross country meet that you were the best runner in the league. You are good, but not that good. You weren't even the best runner on our team. What you did was see the situation and take advantage of the opportunity, which is something a smart runner will do, and you won the race over several superior opponents. That's good, but you might not win another one unless you work harder than everyone else."

"That's not fair!"

"Fair? Life isn't fair, but you make the best of it you can. How much have you grown in the past year?"

"An inch. I'm four foot eleven."

"And you're thirteen years old. You have a natural ability to run, but so does Justine, and she is seven inches taller. She will be our best runner, unless you get serious soon. Plus, you may have been too preoccupied with Justine to see Ferdy breathing down your neck. You can be a top runner, Corey, when you get your growth, since you are good already. If you get complacent, though, you'll never get to the top."

ooo

On the first day of eighth grade, on the way to the cafeteria, the fat hand of the law reached out into the hallway and nabbed me again.

"I am puzzled, Zilch, by the preponderance of perplexity in our pursuits."

"I don't understand what you mean, Sir."

Maybe he had been preparing that line all summer, but he had me stumped. He discarded the "p's" for simple language that a simpleton like me could understand.

"I never caught the smugglers, Zilch, and I think you know the reason why."

Yeesh. I've been found out. I will have to move to Norway with my sister.

"What is that, Sir?"

He took a deep breath, like he was trying to translate his words into a foreign language, found the right word and spoke it: "Probity."

I was wrong. He had been searching the dusty closet of his brain for a discarded p-word. The closet must have been full, because he continued with, "You have paucity in your personality."

"I don't get it."

"Exactly." He bent down to my level and said, "You don't get it because you do not have a talent for subterfuge. You are not good at spying. You are honest."

"Is that bad, Sir?"

"Not bad, just not helpful. However, do not worry. We can fix that."

"But, Mr. Farraday, I thought when the school year ended, I wouldn't need to spy for you anymore. Can't I just go back to being a normal guy?"

"Ha! No student is normal. Just some are stranger than others. You are not released from your obligations until I liberate you. You are my property from now on, if you wish to compete in cross country, that is."

Blackmail.

He gathered his thoughts, reopened the "p" closet, and said, "A principal with principles perseveres in order to prevail over perfidious pupils." Then his face took on the look mine does when I have let go with a long, satisfying burp.

He pushed me into the deep water of Hanway Middle School once again. When I came to the surface and swam past the boy's room, a shark snared me and pulled me back under.

"Give!"

"Come on, Noford," I whined, looking at my shoes. "Can't you let me off the hook?"

"Nope. Long as you're buddy-buddy with the big guy, you're hooked. What's the deal?"

"Just that he still wants to catch you. Maybe you should look for a new line of work."

"Haw! No way. Look at this"

"At this, at this!" buzzed Booger, modeling his new black leather jacket.

I looked up at Noford for the first time. His, which must have cost at least two un-lucky cows their lives, shone like a night full of stars, with silver snaps, buckles, zippers and chains. Two more figures stepped out of the stalls to show me theirs, too.

Yeesh! Not only had the Scuds multiplied, but a girl was in the boys' room. But I couldn't tell which one of the Bosley twins she was.

I stumbled out the door and staggered into the lunchroom. I needed someone normal. I needed my Buds. I found them and gasped, "Bad news!"

Sarah, Hu and Justine, startled, looked up from their Soy Surprise with kidney beans.

"The Bosleys have joined the Scuds. We're four against four now."

"We know," Justine said, "we saw them together in the hallway decked out in their biker costumes. Candy sales must pay well."

Hu said, "This will be an interesting year."

"You can say that again," I muttered.

Hu said, "This will be an interesting year."

Sarah hit him in the nose with a kidney bean.

ooo

Justine was waiting for me after school at the back door. We walked together, toward cross country practice.

"Corey?" she said softly.

"That's me."

"Are we friends now?"

"Sure. We're Buds."

"Do you forgive me for the pranks I pulled on the team last year?"

"Sure. I forgave you last year."

"You know I am going to try to beat you in cross country this year."

"That's okay. Fair and square."

"Right. Friendly competition can make us both better."

"Yes. I want us both to get better."

We were walking side by side around the corner of the school building. She grabbed my hand and whispered in my ear, "Corey, I never thanked you like I should have for helping me out of that jamb and never telling anybody."

What is going on with girls wanting to hold my hand all of the sudden?

I turned to tell her *you're welcome* when she did it without warning. She bent down and kissed me, on the lips, my first kiss from a girl ever.

I had hoped the first would be from Sarah, but I didn't have a choice, did I? Trouble is, I should have turned away, and I just let it happen.

When she was done, I saw a flash of red. Sarah was running away down the sidewalk. Gulp. I told Justine, "Y-y-you're welcome. Don't do that again, okay?"

"Okay."

We didn't speak until we arrived at practice. I was studying the pointed ends of my shoelaces. What are those things called, anyway? A girl's voice said, "Hi, Zip."

A familiar face appeared, one that belonged in the swamps of Fogtown.

"Shelly! What are you doing here?" I sputtered.

"We moved here over the summer. My Dad got a job in the mattress factory. This year we can run on the same team."

"Hey, that's great!"

The two of us had enjoyed running side by side in two meets last year, since we were close to an even match.

Coach began, "School is in, and we have several new recruits with us today. Let me introduce them to you. First, "Shelly Marco…"

We smiled at each other.

"…and her brother, Chad Marco."

I swallowed hard. There he was, the meanest kid in the league last year, the one who licked his lips and called me "hasenpfeffer," the guy who may have cost Cherise the league championship race by pushing her into the underbrush at the last turn. Chad.

While Coach introduced some more sixth and seventh graders, I sidled up and whispered to Shelly, "He's your brother? He doesn't look anything like you."

"Thank heavens," she answered. "We're *fraternal* twins."

10

GIRLS

Coach Rusk sent the seven of us from last year's team through our familiar Butterworth Trail while he kept the "newbies" with him for "the talk." He would lay down the rules, the duties of each runner, the lecture about teamwork and sportsmanship, and, maybe, some basic instruction on running technique. Justine, Shelly and Chad didn't need that last part, but maybe he would use them as examples.

Ferdy and I ran together. Until then I didn't realize how much longer his legs were since last fall. He had gotten faster, not by running faster, but by lengthening his stride. I had to take two steps to his one just to keep even. Would I ever grow?

Ferdy never talked much, but after several minutes he said, "We should run together more often."

"Yeah."

"Maybe run here on Sunday afternoons."

"Yeah."

"Three o'clock?"

"Yeah." Now who was the quiet one?

When we finished, Coach Rusk was about to show the newbies the course and wanted us oldies to join them. "I know

63

some of you are experienced runners and could show off, but I don't want that. We will run together as a team, even though some of you could run faster. We are a team, right?"

"Right!"

So, our seven and their seven ran as one fourteen, slowly. Coach even stopped us at times to explain something, like how to run up a hill and down.

Before practice was over, he had one more point to make. "Part of being a team is to respect those ahead and behind you," he explained, "and to elevate them as well as yourself."

Later, as I jogged up to my house, Dad met me with my orange tee shirt in his hand. Last June he had replaced our neon sweat suits with blazing summer shirts, since orange was "our signature color." Old ladies on porches would set down their iced tea to wave and clap for us. Kids on scooters and big wheels would race us to the end of their block. Dogs would wag their tails. We had become familiar friends. Dad would toss each dog sausage treats. Can dogs see orange?

My father was getting into shape. We could run eight blocks out without slowing down, sit on a bus bench for five minutes, and then run back. This time, when we sunk down for a rest, I asked my father a burning question.

"Dad, did you ever kiss a girl?"

"Let me think, Son. Yes, yes, I think I may have kissed your mother a time or two."

"No, I don't mean Mom. A girl."

"I hate to break it to you, Corey, but..." He put the palm of his hand to my ear and whispered, "...your mother is a girl."

"No, I mean a real girl, like my age, when you were my age."

"Oh, now I get it. You want to kiss Sarah, don't you."

"No ...well ...yes ...but ...no, I had a girl kiss me today. It wasn't Sarah."

"Uh-oh. I see trouble brewing."

"Sarah saw it."

"Uh-oh. Double trouble."

"I didn't mean it. It was an accident."

"So, you're a chick magnet now. The girls can't help themselves."

"It wasn't like that. It was a thank-you kiss."

"Son, there is no such thing as a thank-you kiss."

"What should I do about it?"

"Grovel."

"What does that mean?"

"I am a worm," he mumbled in a non-Dad voice. *"The lowest of the low, I'm sorry, I don't deserve it, but please, please, please forgive me."*

"Does it work?"

"Sometimes, but girls have a strange ability that guys don't have to hear what you are saying between the words, so they know if you really mean what you say. Plus, they never forget anything, so it better never happen again."

"That's hard."

"True, but you'd better learn how to do it if you want a long-term relationship with a girl. Sometimes they want you to be the big strong hero, but other times they need you to be soft and sweet. You're smart if you know when to be which."

ooo

When we got home, both Mom and Sis met us at the door with the look girls get when they are eating chocolate.

"We have a surprise for you."

Oh no, I thought, *most of my surprises lately have not been good ones.*

They ushered us into the living room.

Mom said, "The surprise is in here somewhere. I wonder where it is. Is it behind the sofa? No. Is it in the coat closet?"

She flung open the door. "No. Where is our surprise?"

A muffled giggle came from the area of the picture window. Suddenly, a tiny white tornado spun from behind the drapes, and shrieked, "Surprise!"

Sis, with a flamboyant gesture, announced, "My pleasure is to introduce to you Hermione Ann Dagle, the Princess of the World!"

Hermione was a skinny, tiny, doll-like girl with long white hair. The clue that she had played princess before was when she held her hand out, palm down, and pronounced, "You may kiss my hand."

I'd had enough kissing for one day, but Sis took her up on the offer, and the two of them danced around the room.

Mom explained, "Princess Hermione is going to stay in our castle while her mother visits the land of the hospital. She is three years old."

The little girl put her hands on her hips and glared. "My name is not Her-mi ... Her-mi-o ... It's Annie, and I'm three and a half."

The two girls danced some more while Mom fixed supper. Dad showered upstairs, and I showered in the basement. For the first time I had to slide the bolt across the basement door.

We had not had a foster child since A-lo. The social worker was saving us for emergencies, and none had come up lately. Mom had even gone back to work at Belle's Diner because Belle begged her to, plus Dad said we needed the income. The agreement was that whenever we got another kid, Belle would do her own cooking.

For supper Mom made chicken strips, buttered noodles, and chocolate pudding—a meal for kids. The rest of us did not complain. Between noodle-slurping and spoon-licking, Dad said, "Corey got his first kiss from a girl today."

"Dad!" My face turned tomato red.

Sis looked shocked. "What? You?"

I blurted out, "Dad, that was our secret."

He looked confused. "I thought you would be proud."

Sis asked, "Who? Why?"

Mom said, "My little boy is definitely growing up."

Sis asked, "How much did you have to pay her?"

Dad groaned, "I'm sorry, son. I'm still learning this father thing."

Annie said, "I kiss my mommy. I love my mommy. She has a boo-boo in her tummy. I kissed her tummy. It will get better."

Later, after Hermione was in bed, Mom explained. "Her mother collapsed in a store. They took her in an ambulance to the hospital, and DCFS brought the girl here. Katrina, they call her Kitty, is dehydrated, anemic, and more. They are running tests. They estimate she'll be in the hospital for two weeks."

We all pitched in to make sure the house was safe for a three-year-old, since we had gotten sloppy while we didn't have one.

Several times I caught my sister looking at me funny. She was wondering, I'm sure, why in the world any girl would want to kiss me.

I was wondering the same thing.

11

COLD SPELL

anway School was freezing the next morning. My bones clanged together like wind chimes, and the closer I got to homeroom the worse it felt. Nobody else seemed to notice.

Sarah was staring out the window. Hu was staring at Sarah. When I walked up to her and said, "Hello, Sarah," she kept staring, didn't look, didn't say a word.

When I asked Hu "What is wrong?" he said, "You know." I did know, but I didn't know he knew. I sat at my desk, shivering.

All morning, I wanted to do something about it, but school got in the way. Come lunchtime I was anxious to see Sarah and talk it out. I knew Justine could back me up that it was just a thank-you kiss, and everything would be alright.

Trouble is, to get to lunch you have to pass the principal's office, which is right in the center of the school where all the halls meet, like a guard tower in a prison. The office has four sides looking out at the four halls, and four one-way mirrors make it possible for Mr. Farraday to spy on everything in every direction anytime. I couldn't edge past to escape his claw.

From inside the door, I could see people inches away, girls checking makeup in what they thought was a mirror, boys checking out girls. I turned to the principal for my first lesson in middle school espionage.

"Position your person for perceptivity."

That meant to put yourself where you can see what is going on, and, when you see anything suspicious, report it. Of course, in middle school, everything is suspicious. Choosing what to report would be a challenge, like walking a tightrope over Niagara Falls.

He shoved me back out the door. Rather than getting grabbed again on the way past, I just walked straight to the boys' room. The "Out of Oder" sign hung on the door, so I knew the Scuds were in there, but the "oder" they were out of seemed somehow different. Noford stood inside flanked by the Bosleys. He said, "So what's up now?"

There was no echo a la Booger.

I said, "The principal wants me to report anything suspicious, so, ah, maybe you shouldn't do anything suspicious."

"Haw. Nothin' suspicious here, right T 'n T? We's just honest business owners."

Both nodded yes. I looked at this incredible hulk dressed in black cowskins, and at the dark droids on either side of him. *Nope, nothing strange here at all.*

Noford added, "You should report about today's suspicious lunch. Ugh."

He was right about lunch, which was always mysterious. Then it occurred to me what else was weird about this day— no sign of Booger. You never saw Noford without Booger. Maybe, he was doing some private business in one of the toilet stalls.

❦

69

Surveying the cafeteria, I spotted my Buds in the far corner.

The lunch line was slow because the lunch ladies were ladling steaming green liquid from a bubbling cauldron into cardboard bowls. The menu board said, "seafood ceviche," but we decided it was shark soup, pea green, with weird bits of fish guts swimming to the top, trying to escape, I think. Nobody would have dared eat the glop, except for Booger, and he wasn't in the cafeteria.

I joined my friends. Sarah sat at one end of the table, with Justine at the other end, and Hu in the middle. Nobody was saying anything. I sat like the principal told me to, with my back to the wall (for perceptivity, you know) across from Sarah. She got up and moved over next to Hu. I got up and moved over by Justine. Just then Shelly appeared with her tray and asked, "Can I sit by you, Corey?"

"Sure. This is the Buds' table, and these are my Buds. Hey, everybody, this is my friend Shelly."

"Hi, Buds. I just moved here from Fogerty. I got to know Corey last year in cross country." She sat down by me on the other side from Justine.

Sarah muttered, "Yeah. Corey sure does get around."

I thought I should introduce the Buds to her by name. "Shelly, this is Justine."

"Hi, Justine. I met you at practice yesterday." They leaned forward to smile and finger-wave at each other around me.

"And this is my best friend Hu."

She said, "Hi, Hu," and giggled a little bit, like some girls do sometimes.

"And this is Sarah."

"Pleased to meet you, Shelly," Sarah said with a forced smile. Then she looked at me with a "hmph," picked up her bowl of ceviche and stomped off to throw it in the trash barrel.

"Did I do something wrong?" Shelly wondered.

"No, she's mad at me, not you." I got up to follow Sarah and caught up with her outside the lunchroom door.

"Sarah, we have to talk."

"Hmph."

"Where are you going?"

"Library."

"I know what you saw."

"Sure."

"I didn't mean it."

"Sure."

"It was an accident."

"Sure."

"Will you forgive me?"

"Sure."

"Can we talk about it?"

"We just did."

"Can we talk more?"

"No. Go away."

I went away. Back in the cafeteria my soup was getting cold, but still bubbling, which didn't matter because I wouldn't eat it anyway. I ate my oyster crackers.

Shelly, being new and uninformed, took a spoonful of the fishtail soup, then spit it back out. "Is the food here always this bad?"

"No," answered Hu, "sometimes it's worse."

"How could it be worse?"

"Try it tomorrow," he said.

"You could thank my mother," Justine said. "She considers the school cafeteria her laboratory and the students her caged rats. She thinks this food is her greatest accomplishment in life, her 'claim to fame,' she says. She wants no Hanway student to be fat."

"It's working," said Hu, pushing the bowl to the far corner

of the table.

Justine shrugged. "If you'd been dragged by her into all the fancy bistros I have, you would know our cooks got it wrong. Ceviche is served cold, and the fish is supposed to be raw."

"Yuck. That *would* be worse. I guess I could bring my lunch from home," Shelly said.

"No, you can't," Hu informed her. "The school confiscates any food you bring in. The only food allowed in the school is what the lunch ladies serve. Actually, if you bring something from home that they like, the teachers take it from you and eat it in the teachers' lounge."

The cafeteria has four trash barrels in the four corners. Each one had a line of about twenty people dumping their full bowls of soup. Suddenly a rumbling came from the barrels, growing louder and louder, like they say a tornado sounds, but with a gurgling, like your stomach makes when you have the flu.

My Buds and I hit the floor and crawled under the table.

I looked over at the kids in the trash line, who were scared but too stubborn to give up their chance to get the slop du jour out of sight. The line grew longer—but faster—as they threw in bowl after bowl and ran for cover.

Then the unthinkable happened. Each trash barrel developed spasms, which became a full-blown seizure and upchucked chunks of green slime. It bounced off the ceiling and walls and floors. The victims in the trash line were green from head to foot, running blindly in circles. The slime spread like liquid fire across the floor.

I rolled out, jumped up and felt stickiness surging across my feet.

If you ever saw that old black and white movie on cable called *The Blob,* which my dad made me watch, because he said it was "a hoot," you knew what to do.

Run for it!

I slid across the floor like on ice and turned to look.

Goo was blowing from the barrels, oozing into every crack in the floor, pulsing like it was alive, chasing the lunch ladies out of the kitchen, and devouring everything in its path. The place emptied in about thirty seconds, except for those who got plastered with it. They screamed, "It's eating my face!" It took about forty seconds for them to feel their way out the door.

The Bosley twins, though, seemed to have no fear. They appeared in the doorway with smart phones from somewhere and filmed the whole thing.

I perceptivized it, as I had been instructed, then tried to stamp the goo off in the hallway, but it wouldn't let go. As soon as I could, I slogged to Principle Farraday's office, leaving a green trail all the way.

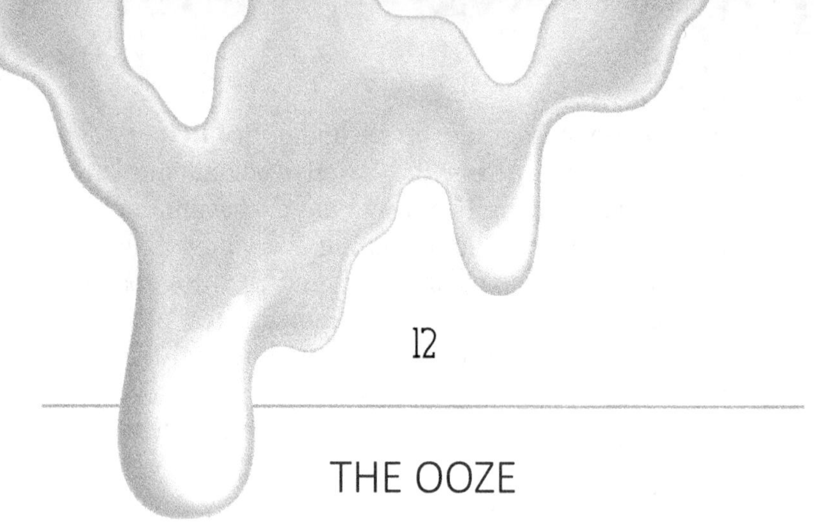

12

THE OOZE

Never before had I dared to open the door to the principal's hideout. I stood there, green ooze licking at my ankles, took a deep breath, eased it open a crack, slipped in, and eased it shut. With the dictionary open on his desk, Principal Farraday was mouthing words to himself. He seemed not to notice the commotion in the hallway, or me, until he said without looking up, "What do you want?"

"They got the soup wrong," I told him.

He looked up, looked down at the book, and said, "Preposterous."

I answered, "Justine Highcourt, who knows these things, said that ceviche is served cold, not hot, and the fish in it is supposed to be raw, not cooked."

He looked up and said, "Perplexing."

"Well, you told me to report what seems suspicious. Is it okay that the lunchroom is oozing green glop and it's spreading down the hall this way?"

"What?"

He sprung from his chair to spy through the window. "Oh.

74

Oh? Oh!" He began in a shout. "You did properly to report promptly. The polluted area will need to be quarantined until the problem is probed and the determinant agent investigated. Why am I telling you this?"

He waddled to the phone and called 911. "Hanway School. Help!" He slammed down the receiver, turned on the speaker system, grabbed the microphone and announced, "Pupils and personnel, evacuate the building. This is an emergency, not a drill. Do it now." He lowered the mike, thought again, raised it, and yelled, "Orderly, please. Do not panic!"

The thundering herd shook the building.

He took a deep breath. "Promptly prepare to propel your persons from the property upon perceiving the pinging of the, ah, the, ah, alarm. Tomorrow, prepare your personal packaged provisions for, ah, lunch. Please, ah, please, ah, phooey! It's coming this way. Get out, quick!"

Then he broke the glass cage inside his office, yanked the fire alarm down, picked up his coffee mug and his dictionary, and fled for the door.

Fire drills are ordinary. Green globs from outer space do not come every day. Cheering all the way, the kids stormed the exits, teachers in the mix. The Scuds were the last ones out. They were dragging two heavy gym bags on wheels.

The police came first, then the fire trucks, the ambulances, the tow trucks, the utility vans, the lawyers, and the dog catcher. Everything with sirens and everyone who chased sirens came at once. The teachers couldn't even drive their cars out of the lot to flee for McDonald's. Within ten minutes of the evacuation the Scuds sold out their entire candy supply. The whole crowd had Snickers and Butterfingers.

Turns out the slime didn't eat faces or other body parts. Nobody was hurt except for bruises. They just looked like slimy green Martians.

The students, who had hidden their cell phones in pockets and backpacks, texted their parents, took videos, and sent them to YouTube.

When the bus drivers, roused from their mid-day slumbers, arrived to load up the students to haul them home, there was nowhere for them to park. They opened the bus doors out on the streets, but nobody got on. Slime or not, this was too exciting to leave.

DANGER ⚠ HAZARDOU

When the HAZMAT truck arrived, it spun across the football field to the back, leaving deep gouges in the turf. The first responders unloaded the gear, pulled on spacesuits, and approached the building. I know. I squeezed around the corner to watch. They flung open the doors. The green blob tried to get out. They slammed the doors shut again and went back for rubber hip boots.

When I came back to the front I could see Sarah's red waterfall of hair in the distance, climbing into her mom's car. I wanted to explain to her what happened with Justine, I really did, but no way could I get to her through the mob. So, I went back to stand beside Principal Farraday. I think I felt sorry for him.

A young woman in jeans and a t-shirt that said, "LAURA FOUNTAIN LIVE!" was running up to us at full speed. I wondered if she was worried that a little sister had been eaten by the green monster, until I saw a clipboard in one hand and a phone in the other.

She took three deep breaths then spoke. "I am Laura Fountain from the Hanway Herald. Can I get your perspective on this tragedy, Principal Farty?"

"Now, Miss Faucet," he said, "I would not call this a tragedy, just a minor incident in the life of a wonderful school. And my name is Farraday. F-a-r-r-a-d-a-y."

She blushed and wrote it down.

"Sorry. I just left another interview about the Rest Stop Robbers hitting again, so I am out of sorts. May I interview you?"

When he nodded, she punched a few things on her phone and held it out.

"I do not perceive who is the perpetrator of this practical joke, but they will be punished properly. This perceptive pupil ..." (He put his hand on my shoulder. It felt like Noford's, so I backed away.) "... pointed out the problem to me."

The reporter saw me for the first time and said, "Oh, I thought that might be your grandson from Hanway Elementary. I'll get to him in a minute."

One thing I knew was I did *not* want her to get to me. Besides I was afraid of the permanent possibility of "p" poisoning, so I backed into the crowd.

When Laura Fountain rushed away, probably to meet her deadline for the next day's paper, another noise zeroed in, along with a stiff wind, from both sides.

Two helicopters soared into sight, aiming at each other before peeling off.

From the east, *WHAM Hard Hitting News* buzzed the school and hovered above the HAZMAT guys as they unloaded giant vacuum cleaners from a semi that had dug more tire trenches in the football field. From the west *KAYO, the Pride of the Prairie,* took pictures of the crowd as they scattered to let the copter land. I'm sure by six o'clock we would look like we were all fleeing the Blob in terror. The only one to stand his ground was our principal, like the captain of a sinking ship.

They interviewed him, p-words and all, but I couldn't hear it over the sound of the other whirlybird touching down. While KAYO argued with the cops and the HAZMAT chief over whether they could go inside, I saw a WHAM reporter and a camera woman sneak in an open window. For the first time ever, Hanway School would be famous for something.

By the time all the students and the teachers and the whirlybirds went away, it was three o'clock. Only the slime and the toxic waste crew were left behind. Principal Farraday and I stood alone outside the school. I was waiting for cross country practice. He was waiting for an angry school board to come for an emergency meeting.

He said to me, "The professional preparers ... oh, forget it ... the school cooks said they had to boil the soup to meet the state health code. Mrs. Percival, our science teacher, calls it a normal chemical reaction, an entirely natural phenomenon."

I responded, "That stuff sure looked alive to me."

ooo

I was the only runner who showed up. Since Coach Rusk didn't work at the school he hadn't heard about the ooze. I told him.

"Unbelievable," he said. "I heard the sirens, but I didn't look, and my cell phone doesn't get a signal in the basement. Where the church is, downtown, we hear sirens all the time. We don't pay much attention."

"Nobody's here. Should I go home, too?"

"Actually, Corey, you could help me get a little work done on our trail."

In the church van he had a stack of wooden signs, seven

fence posts, a post hole digger, a toolbox and a bucket of nuts and bolts.

"Our cross country league has new rules this year," he explained, "so to meet league standards, we need to install permanent directional signs in Butterworth Park. You can help me."

We bolted the signs to the posts, dug holes, dropped the posts in, refilled the holes, stomped the dirt down, and went on to the next fork or corner of the trail, seven in all. We were quiet for a while before Coach said, "What's on your mind, Corey?"

"How did you know?"

"You brood, Corey. Anybody who knows you knows you brood."

"I don't want to talk about it."

"Yes, you do. I can tell. Is it the same thing that upset you at camp?"

"Some of it, yes, but my life has gotten even messier."

"Tell me about it."

"I told my dad, and he told my whole family. You won't tell anyone else, will you?"

"I promise I won't."

"Sarah's mad at me."

"Why?"

"Justine kissed me."

"Uh-oh."

"It was an accident."

"Nobody kisses by accident."

"I didn't know Justine was going to, but she just did. Sarah saw it. She won't talk to me."

"I'm not surprised."

"What should I do?"

"Have you apologized?"

"Yeah. I asked her to forgive me, and she said 'sure,' but

she still won't talk to me."

"Corey, she didn't mean, 'Sure, I forgive you.' She meant, 'Sure, if you think you're going to get off that easy, you've got another thing coming.'"

"Girls are hard to understand," I complained. "Justine said she kissed me to say thank you for my helping her with her prankster thing last year, but my Dad says there is no such thing as a thank-you kiss, and if he's right I don't know why she did it, and I don't understand why it made Sarah mad, since she said she can't be my girlfriend, because she wants to stay friends, and I don't even know why they both like me."

"Maybe that's the reason they like you."

"Huh?"

"Never mind. Just keep apologizing until she does forgive you. I think she will. But don't let it happen again."

"That's not all," I said, and I told him everything. Some of it was old stuff, some was new. It just poured out like the s-s-s-s-s-s of a bike tire with a pin hole—the Buds, the Scuds, Principal Farraday, the orange shirts and the grandmas waving from their porches, A-lo and Annie, the mice in the basement, everything—until I had no air left in me to leak out.

As we finished the last signpost, Coach said, "You're right. Your life is complicated. I'll help you as much as I can, but you need more help than mine. Can I pray for you?"

"Sure." I thought a second, then added, "I mean, sure, you can pray for me, because I need all the help I can get."

So, he did.

I thought he meant he would pray for me in his prayers at bedtime, which I think all pastors are supposed to do, but he meant right then. He prayed for me in Butterworth Park, under a maple tree, out loud. As far as I know no one had ever prayed for me before. If they did, I never heard it before. It was like having your flat bike tire patched and pumped back up.

As we put the tools away, my dad roared up in the old

Durango, his orange shirt glowing, even in the daylight.

"There you are, Corey, your mother is worried sick about you. We thought you might have been eaten up by the Ooze. Everybody is talking about the Ooze."

"I'm okay. I was just helping Coach Rusk fix the cross country trail."

Coach shook my father's hand through the car window. "I'm Barney Rusk, Corey's coach. I've seen you but haven't met you. I didn't know you hadn't heard from him."

"I'm Robert Zilch, Barney. You can call me Bob. My wife and I didn't hear about the Ooze until we got home from work and turned on the news. When our boy didn't come home, we panicked. You should have called, Corey."

"On what? You don't let me have a cell phone, and I couldn't go back into the school."

"You should have come home."

"It was cross country practice time."

Coach spoke up in my defense. "I apologize, Bob. I should have sent him home, but I want to compliment you on the character of your son. He is a fine young man."

Young man? That was another first for me.

My father said, "Thank you, Barney. We are doing our best. By the way, the School Board has cancelled school for the rest of the week."

That didn't mean much, since tomorrow was Friday, but you take what you can get. Maybe Sarah would cool off by Monday.

ooo

When we got home supper was ready, macaroni and cheese with hot dog bites mixed in. More kid food for Annie. She was bouncing in her booster seat, making siren sounds.

"Guess what? We saw fire trucks an' am-bu-lan-cers an' po-lice cars. Whoooo-yoooo-wooooo."

Sis said, "I'm jealous, Corey. Nothing exciting ever

81

happens in high school, not that I want to go backward, of course. But we have school tomorrow, and you don't."

"Tough luck," I said.

Mom looked glum. "Speaking of tough luck, Kitty is in intensive care."

Annie gushed, "Kitty is my mommy. She's in 'tense care to get better. She's gonna come get me an' take me to our house."

"Not for a while, Annie. She's not all the way better yet."

"Mommy's sick in her tummy. I kissed it. I miss my mommy." She began to cry, climbed down and ran to her bedroom. Mom and Dad followed her, which left Sis and I alone.

"That's bad, isn't it, intensive care?" I asked.

"Yes. It isn't good."

"What's wrong with her?"

"They haven't told us yet. Maybe they don't know yet."

"Then how can they fix it?"

"I don't know. So, this Ooze thing, were you trapped in the middle of it?"

"More than you'll ever know."

"Was it, like, hungry?"

Okay, I would have to tell her, or she would never shut up. So, I described it, maybe even made up a little bit extra about it, until she seemed satisfied enough to change the subject.

"Did Justine kiss you again today?"

"No!"

"Did Sarah?"

"No, she won't even talk to me."

"Oh, really? That means she likes you."

"I don't know why."

My sister said, "Neither do I."

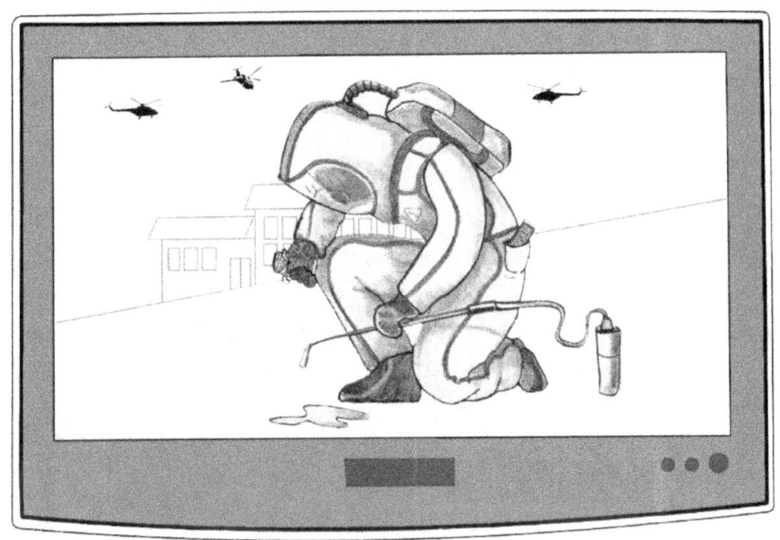

13

WHAT'S NEWS?

Macaroni and cheese is easy to eat, and fast. It slides down like ... never mind.

Dad was in a hurry to watch the news. Since he had missed the ooze in person, he had to fill that void.

No TV station is anywhere close to Hanway, or wants to be, but we get both WHAM and KAYO news from afar at five o'clock. Dad seldom watches it because he says, "I don't want to know about life in the big city." A "big" city is anything bigger than Hanway.

WHAM's helicopter must be fast, because they led off their news with, "A small town made big news today. The aliens arrived in the rural school of Hanway at noon today, wreaking havoc, and I mean reeking. The smell was horrendous, like rotten fish.”

Showing on the screen, aerial view, were the HAZMAT droids storming the back doors in full outer-space regalia (Sarah's word), then panning to the emergency vehicles in the front of the school and the enormous crowd with their heads down. They may have been trying to avoid the headwinds of the whirling helicopters, but I think they were eating candy bars.

The talking head said, “The poor principal was too perplexed to speak rationally, but we got the real scoop, and we mean scoop.”

The screen showed a reporter slogging down the clogged green hallway, saying into her microphone, “This is the end of these new shoes. I'll go home barefoot. Whatever this stuff is, it sticks and though it is no longer spreading, it still seems alive. We are now approaching the school cafeteria, the epicenter of the eruption. According to our sources…” She lifted the smart phone in her left hand. “…some kind of bombs, planted by aliens or maybe terrorists, exploded from the garbage cans, spurting slime all around the room.”

The screen flashed to a telephoto video of kids crying, coated with green goo, trying to get their mothers to hug them, but being kept at arms' length. Then it flashed back to the lunchroom ceiling, still dripping. The reporter, with an “eek,” jumped back from being slimed.

“According to our latest information, the Inland Security Department has been called. We will have a follow-up story tomorrow. For now … let's just get out of here!”

Dad switched channels to KAYO, and we heard them saying, “The brutal Rest Stop Robbers are still at large, terrorizing three states. Speaking of terror, from another neighboring state, aliens have landed in the remote hamlet of Hanway, while the citizens flee."

I was right; the video from overhead *did* look like we were fleeing an attack of Martians when we were really just fleeing the blades of the landing helicopter.

"Green globs of The Ooze from Outer Space invaded Hanway Middle School. Speculation has already flooded the internet that this is an initial experiment for aliens to take over larger centers of population and cripple the world's communication grid."

Principal Farraday's red face appeared on the screen as he launched two states into his world of p-words. I couldn't hear it because my whole family was laughing so hard.

At six o'clock, believe it or not, the national news lead story was Hanway. We were definitely famous. The story was the same, just in a more professional way. But the video was of the Ooze as it was happening, seen from the doorway of the lunchroom, in living color. I wondered how much money the Scuds were paid for *that* video.

When Coach Rusk called our house that night to say, "be at Butterworth tomorrow for practice," I asked him to pray for Kitty Dagle in Hanway Hospital. Maybe if God wouldn't listen to my prayers for her, he would listen to Coach's, with him being a pastor and all.

ooo

The next day the fish-soup jokes were flowing as we gathered for practice.

What will win the war against obesity? Fish soup.

What is causing global warming? The Ooze.

What is faster than a speeding bullet? Super-ceviche!

Okay, I didn't say they were good jokes. Coach even told

us to "run like the Ooze is gaining on you."

We did.

The fear was still fresh.

After that, he shared the new, improved league rules. Besides the new signposts, we would need to cut the brush back, because the trails needed to be widened to allow more runners at a time, ten from each team. Also, the host team would be required to hire two league-approved officials, one at the start and finish, and one floating along the course to call fouls. A foul would disqualify the runner from that race.

"These rules will make for better meets and will improve our team's chances, since so many of you are good runners. I think we could win two or three meets this year. Our first meet will be a week from today at Old Humphrey. So, let's work hard and be ready. Not all of you have turned in your medical permission forms. We need them before that first meet."

Yeesh! Dr. Cold Hands, here I come.

Coach sent us through the course again. Justine and Shelly ran ahead of me, chatting and laughing like old friends. Suddenly I felt an elbow in my ribs and heard a grunt from behind.

"Move over, Zippo," Chad sneered and dug the elbow in. "Thought you were going to be the big cheese this year, didn't ya. Well, I eat cheese for breakfast."

I responded, "Why don't you guzzle fish soup instead."

"This is a warning, Zippo. I'm gonna scramble you like eggs with cheese on top."

"Hungry, are you, Chaddo?"

"Yup, and when I'm thirsty, I'll suck your blood."

Same old bully. This will be an interesting season.

At four-thirty, as I started running home, I was flanked by Justine and Shelly. Chad was off somewhere tearing legs off spiders. Justine blew me a kiss (which I dodged) and peeled off to her house. Shelly stayed with me until three blocks from my house where a new apartment complex had one building finished.

"This is my place while we look for a house," she said.

We stopped running and sat down in the grass.

"Corey, is it okay for me to sit with you and Justine at lunchtime? I don't want to eat alone, but I don't want to butt in if I'm not wanted."

"You don't want to sit with your brother Chad?"

"I'd rather eat fish soup."

"It's okay with my friends, I'm sure. They'll be nice to you. We call ourselves the Buds."

"Justine and Hu seem to accept me, but I'm not sure about Sarah."

"Sarah will come around. She's mad at me, not you."

"Does Hu have a girlfriend?"

I had never thought about that. "I don't think so. He doesn't have much time for girls since he has to work after school every day at the Peking Pagoda."

"Oh, well, I think he's cute."

ooo

When I got home, Dad and Mom were gone to the hospital to see Kitty, and Sis was playing dolls with Annie.

After my shower, Mom was back in the kitchen making spaghetti. Standing in the doorway, I asked, "Is Kitty okay?"

"Not yet, dear. She's holding her own." Mom's eyes got all drippy. "It's so sad. They don't usually let strangers into intensive care, but she has no family,

nobody at all. So, they thought it would do her good to have visitors."

"What's she like, Mom?"

"A paper doll, honey, she's a paper doll."

"Paper dolls?" A little voice chirped behind me. "Mommy and I play with paper dolls. Can we? Can we?"

Sis hustled Annie away, saying, "I've got paper dolls from when I was a little girl. Let's go find them."

Later, after supper, when Annie was in bed, Sis asked, "Is Annie's mother going to die?"

"Don't say that!" Mom gasped. "No. She can't die."

"But if she does, can we keep Annie?"

"Don't even think it."

"But Mom, Annie wouldn't have a family. Everybody needs a family."

✹✹✹

When Dad opened the paper after supper, the lead story was the Ooze. Laura Fountain had not made the press deadline the night before, so she made up for it with a feature, including pictures and stuff she must have gotten from YouTube. Dad was getting a big kick out of it. Suddenly he went silent.

"Corey, how did you get in here?"

"What? I didn't!"

"Yes, you did. It says, 'Principal Fairly gives credit to a student, Corey Zilch, who alerted him to the disaster before any of the students were injured.'"

My parents looked at me strangely. My sister said, "You?"

I had been noticed again. *Yeesh!*

But on Monday in school, nobody made a big deal of it. Either nobody reads the paper, or nobody remembered who Corey Zilch was from my brief time of fame last year.

Saturday a thunderstorm blew through and washed out practice. Sunday, Ferdy and I ran together through Butterworth's high school trail, not saying a word. Ferdy listened to his iPod, while I listened to my thoughts. At the end, Ferdy sighed. "Thanks, Corey. I get lonesome running by myself. My dad and I used to run together. I miss him."

I should appreciate having a family.

I said, "We can do this every Sunday."

"Cool."

Before I even reached my homeroom on Monday the Scuds had me in their office. They didn't need a sign. They owned the boys' room now. Everybody used the other one.

"Hey, Zippinator," roared Noford, "you's the best!" The Bosleys stood on either side of him like statues. "You's one of us now, dude. How'dya do it?"

"Do what?"

"How'd you make that ooze stuff? You da man, Zilch! We made a couple hundred bucks, and we got a day off school. I owe ya big, man. What'dya want, a share of the loot?"

"No, but maybe I'll need a favor some time, okay?"

"Okay. But don't let on that we's friends, ya know. Works better if nobody figures it out."

"Fine with me," I said.

The cafeteria was closed, with DANGEROUS-DO-NOT-CROSS tape all over the door. We all ate bag lunches from home in the hallways. Noford started an auction.

"I got PB&J. Do I hear a dollar? Yes. Two dollars. Yes. Two twenty-five. Yes. Two fifty. Sold for two-fifty.

"Next, double-chocolate brownies, with nuts, starting at two dollars ..."

Everybody was selling and buying and eating what they wanted. Hanway School hadn't had such a food feast for at least two years, and all the time Principal Farraday just watched from the office. I think he knew that, if he stopped the bidding, he would have a riot on his hands, more headlines in tomorrow's Hanway Herald and another school board meeting. A bunch of kids had brought extra stuff while it was legal—to hide in their lockers for future snacks—but they used the auction to double or triple their money. The Scuds got a chunk of the profit.

The Buds ate at our second favorite meeting place, the water fountain. We all brought our favorites. I had cold toasted cheese, Hu had a big bag of wontons, Sarah had a turkey and cheese Lunchable, and Justine ate a cucumber and ketchup sandwich on rye bread. Shelly sold her dollar-sized maple pancakes for three bucks, bought low in the crowd, sold high in the auction, and parlayed her lunch into a baloney sandwich and twenty dollars profit, minus Noford's commission. That got Hu's attention, let me tell you.

As for Noford, I was amazed. He couldn't be that smart, could he? He must have cleared another two hundred just on lunch, and he saved his candy bars for selling in the hallway between classes.

14

BOOGERLESS

Booger Schmidt was gone, vanished from the face of the earth. You don't know what you've got till it's gone.

The first day we had returned to school the kids sniffed the air like, "Something is different." The second day they looked around like, "This doesn't seem like our school anymore." The third day the evidence of antiseptic was almost gone, but it still didn't smell normal. The fourth day even Principal Farraday noticed a difference. He told me, "Something weird is going on here. You need to find out what has changed."

I thought it would be weird be if nothing was weird, but I said, "Yes, Sir."

The "Out of Oder" sign on the bathroom was gone. Boys still didn't dare go in, but they could breathe better as they snuck past. New kinds of school smells could be detected and even enjoyed. The girls who doused themselves with Eau de Flambe got noticed at last. The jocks-who-never-changed-their-socks exuded the lock-er room aroma they loved and were admired for what they were—athletes with the feet to prove it.

Some still thought the improvement could be traced to the detox of the cafeteria, but those of us in the know knew it was the fine fragrance of Boogerlessness.

On Wednesday, Principal Farraday cut the ribbons and herded the student body into the new "dining area." We could no longer bring lunch bags and negotiate for the best deal. He should have passed out sunglasses. The walls were bright white instead of sick green. All the burned out or buzzing light tubes had been replaced with LED. You felt like you were in the spotlight on the stage of a high school musical. Twenty years of gooey scum had been buffed off the stainless-steel serving kiosks, which reflected the lights so glaringly that you had squint as you slid past the food. Even the new garbage containers had a new-car smell.

Principal Farraday announced, "In recognition of the remarkable refurbishment of our room of repast, your reward will be ..." With a Vanna White sweep of the arm, he pulled down the drop cloth over the menu board, which contained a word we had never seen there before. "... real pizza!"

A sound never heard before arose from the ranks, like the continent of Atlantis rising again from the sea.

Applause!

True, the crust was gluten free, the sauce was pomegranate rather than tomato, and the pepperoni was turkey, but no one complained. The garbage cans kept their pleasant aroma for one more day. Nothing was tossed away but bare plates and napkins.

Around the table the Buds speculated about the fate of Booger Schmidt. The consensus was that Booger—the only person in school who always ate the cafeteria food—had eaten the ceviche and had exploded, so the real reason for the decontamination of the lunchroom was to erase all traces of Booger. I guess that they forgot he was already gone that day.

The good part was that the Buds were complete, and Sarah was talking, though not yet to me. During study hall later I found her in the library reading Shakespeare.

I sidled up to her and whispered, "Hi, Sarah."

She glanced up from *As You Like It* and back down. "Corey."

"We have to talk."

"Sure."

"You have to forgive me."

"Sure."

"I'm really sorry."

"Sure."

"Enough of the sure!"

Heads turned. The librarian shushed me.

I whispered, "It just happened. It wasn't planned."

"Okay."

"She kissed me. I didn't kiss her back."

"But you didn't stop her, did you?"

"No."

"And you enjoyed it, didn't you?"

"No. Well, sort of. Yes, I guess."

"Okay."

"It didn't mean anything."

"Okay."

"It won't happen again."

"Corey, I like you as a boy."

That's good, I thought, since I am a boy, and she is a girl, and I like her as a girl, too. That gives me hope.

"What I am afraid of is that you will turn into a man."

"Well, yes," I said, "I plan to do that."

"All the things you just said, all your excuses for kissing Justine, are the same things I hear my father saying to my mother when they have their fights. Still, he keeps doing the same stuff, over and over. I don't want you to be like my dad."

"I won't. I promise."

"How do I know I can trust you?"

"I don't know. Just keep watching me, I guess, until you believe me."

"Okay. You are on probation for now. If you ever do it again, I warn you, I will call a meeting of the Buds and make the motion to throw you out."

"Can we still be friends?"

"I guess."

ooo

Hermione—Annie—was not a picky eater as long as it was something she liked. Supper that night was toasted cheese sandwiches with bits of tomato and bacon in them. She loved it, ate a whole one, and half of my sister's. I ate two.

Dad said, carefully, "We are planning to visit a certain medical facility on Saturday, but don't spill the beans."

"Ick," declared Annie, "I don't like beans."

Dad continued. "A certain person is in a regular room now and asking to see a small person. We thought we could venture there together as a family."

I spoke up. "Dad, I want to meet her, I really do, but I have to run cross country. Our first meet is in Old Humphrey this Saturday."

"Then I guess we will go without you."

Mom changed the subject. "Corey, I got you an appointment with Dr. Collins after school tomorrow. You will need to run straight home instead of going to your practice."

"E-e-y-e-w." Sis scrunched up her face, "Dr. Cold Hands

again." She shivered.

Mom said, "That isn't very nice, Sissy. You should be respectful."

"Do you respect him, Mom?"

"No, I guess not, but at least we don't have to wait a month for an appointment."

"I'll need to tell Coach Rusk," I said.

"I called him already a few minutes ago. He okayed it."

After supper I was reading *The History of the American Colonies*, about how they treated sick people by getting leeches to suck their blood, and how they killed George Washington by sucking too much of his blood. I wondered when and where Dr. Cold Hands had gotten his doctor training. I thought I knew who did the blood sucking for him.

15

NORMAL

The Buds returned to near normal on Thursday. The Scuds, on the other hand, would never be normal. The menu was back to its abnormal self, with ground lima bean patties on a turnip bun. As I paid $2.50 for the privilege of being a white rat in Mrs. Highcourt's laboratory, I spied abnormality multiplied at the Scuds' table—one, two, three, four, five. No Booger, but the Incredible Hulk and Goth Girl had enlisted.

At the Buds' table, I poked my thumb toward the Scuds. "What's up with that?"

"We were wondering, too," said Hu.

"I can help with that," Shelly offered. "The Shrek in the green shirt? That's my brother Chad, but I don't know the girl."

"What's Chad doing there?" Sarah asked.

"Making friends with his own kind. I choose you, and he chooses them."

"I'll find out who the girl is," I said, and went over. I stared Goth Girl in the face, and the light dawned. I used to think she was mousy.

Noford growled, "Get outta here, bug, or I'll squash ya." But he gave me a wink.

Back at the Buds' table, I said, "I know who it is."

Hu interrupted me. "Don't tell us. We have a theory. Hear us out and see if we're right."

Justine apparently was elected spokesperson. "We think the Goth girl is Booger Schmidt, who was in the hospital having a sex-change operation, got a tattoo, and came back Goth. While he was in the hospital, they disinfected him. Are we right?"

"Wrong. The girl is Amy, the girl who ran the candy operation last year. She got sent to Juvie, came back as a cast member from iCarly, and now she remade herself as Wednesday from the Addams Family. I think Amy plans to be an actor."

"Wow," exclaimed Sarah, "what a life!"

I think she was a little jealous.

She went on, "That might explain where Noford got the auction idea. She's smart."

Shelly said, "Hanway is a more interesting school than Fogtown ever was."

Hu was curious. "Why did you move from there to Hanway?"

"Because of the recession and a bad crop of beans last year, we couldn't pay the bills on our farm. The bank called in the loan. So, we are selling the farm, and my father got a job in the mattress factory. I guess people still have to sleep when the economy is bad. When we sell the farm, we should have enough left to buy a place. I hate living in an apartment."

"My dad works in the mattress factory," I said.

"My dad is the production manager," Justine added.

"Is it a good place?" Shelly asked.

I said, "I think so. I never asked."

Shelly said, "Father hates being cooped up, but we won't

know until the bills are paid whether we'll be living in a house or a trailer."

Justine said, "Don't move to the trailer park where Booger Schmidt lives ... used to live."

Shelly continued, "I'm okay with living in the city. I never was much into the farm."

"What about your brother?" Sarah asked.

"He misses it bad. He especially liked wrestling with the young pigs, and the butchering. He loved the butchering."

"E-e-e-y-e-w," we all said at once.

As we left for classes, Hu told me, "I miss the two of us doing things together like we did last summer. Could you come to my house for Sunday dinner and maybe we can play a game or something?"

"Yeah, I miss that, too. I'm sure my parents will let me come."

To tell you the truth, I looked forward to eating more real Chinese food almost as much as being with my best friend.

Dr. Collins' office was as cold as ever. At her desk, Nurse Bulger was filing her claws to a point. "You again," she grumped. "Didn't you come last year?"

"Yeah, I was here."

"I thought you were dying of something."

"Nope, I just needed my sports physical."

"Wait here. The doctor is occupied."

She filed her file, levitated from her chair, shuffled to the mini-frig, took a big swig of her potion, scratched the hair on her chin, and adjusted the Doctor diploma on the wall. I could see the date: 1959.

"Mom," I whispered. "You don't need to go with me this year. I'm not scared ... much."

"Growing up, huh?"

A yell spilled from the torture chamber and splashed into the outer room. "Cubs win! Cubs win!" A minute later Dr. Cold Hands stuck his head out the door and said, "I can see you now, Corky."

I went in alone, except for Nurse Bulger. She wasn't a problem, even when I stripped to my undershorts. She had her nose in a paperback called *Philo, the Passionate Vampire*, and never even looked up.

The doctor asked, "How are we feeling today, Corky?"

I didn't know how he was feeling, but his hands hadn't touched my skin yet, so I said, "I'm Corey. I'm feeling fine."

"That's too bad. We'll see what we can do about that." He pulled on some too-small plastic gloves, so it took a while, which gave him time to explain, "The state makes me wear these darned things because of the finger fungus, you know."

Yeesh.

He grabbed my throat and squeezed; his hands cold even through the gloves. "No lumps. No mumps," he muttered. He put a stethoscope against my chest. I jumped. He mumbled, "Still beating. Good. A bit fast, though."

"So, Corky, how old are you now? Ten?"

"Corey. Thirteen."

"That's what I thought. Have you been checked for dwarfism?"

"No."

"That's all right. Too late anyway."

He took one of those little lights they use to look up your nose and flicked the switch. Nothing. "Nurse, do we have any batteries?"

"Nope."

He held up two fingers. "How many?"

"Two," I answered.

"No, there's ..." He looked down at his hand. "Oh, yes, two. Open your mouth." He looked. "You have all your teeth. Can you swallow?"

"Yes."

"Too bad. Let's try it and see. Nurse, what do you have for this girl to swallow?"

She fished in her pocket and found something small and black. I hoped it was a raisin.

"Swallow this," he commanded.

I did.

"How does that feel, Corky?"

"Fine. My name is Corey, and I am a thirteen-year-old *boy*."

"That's too bad. Reminds me of those twins I had in here last week. Hard to tell sometimes. People make strange children nowadays. Glad I never had any. How are your reflexes?"

Without waiting for an answer, he snatched a shiny metal pan from the counter and dropped it on the floor. CLANG.

Nurse Bulger didn't flinch. I kicked with both legs,

connecting with Dr. Cold Hands in two soft places. Mom rushed through the door. "What the ...?"

The doctor, bent over, croaked, "Reflexes good."

Nurse Bulger spoke without looking up. "Three weeks and we retire. I found a home that'll take him. I'll move to Salem. I can't wait to get back to Salem." She smiled like a wolf.

Mom fumbled in her purse for the form and a pen, handing it to Dr. Cold Hands. "Sign this form, please."

He looked at it. "Sports, huh. Baseball?"

"No. Cross country."

"What country?"

"Zimbabwe."

"That's what I thought," he said and signed.

"What do I owe you?" Mom asked.

"Free. We can't charge while we're being sued," answered Nurse Bulger. "Have a nice Halloween. I plan to."

The doctor waved from a half-bent position. "Bye, bye, Corky. Hope you get over what you've got."

On the way out, Mom whispered, "I'll fill out the rest of the form when we get home."

"Mom, can we get a new doctor?"

16

OLD HUMPHREY

Coach Rusk gathered the team at the school at 8:30 Saturday morning, even if the parents were driving them to Old Humphrey. All the kids had rides except for me, Ferdy, and a new sixth grader named Rory Jones.

The kids whose parents came had to introduce them to the group. Betty Jean seemed proud of her biker dad and tattooed mom. Justine's father was with her, but her mother stayed home. Shelly and Chad's parents resembled them, Shelly's mom wiry like her and her dad like a bull, even more muscled and mean-looking than Chad.

Coach filled in the parents and grandparents on what he expected of all the runners and on the league rules, like that only ten could run at each meet. One sixth grade girl had quit the team, saying, "This is just too much work," so three would have to sit out the first race. He emphasized that all runners must be present, unless excused by him, even if they were not running, because "we are a team, and we are all in this together."

He continued, "For home meets, runners will be in Butterworth Park an hour before starting time, for stretching,

102

warm-ups, and a team huddle. A team member who does not properly warm up will not run that day. For away meets, allow an extra thirty minutes for a jog through the course, so you have no surprises to slow you down.

"We really appreciate your support of this team. Cross country doesn't have the pizzazz of football, so most of our fans are from your families, except for the conference meet at the end of the season, which draws a crowd. Please come as often as you can.

"Cross country is a healthier sport for your young people, and a better preparation for life. Life is not a game, but an endurance race. Winning is nice when it happens, but the real satisfaction is in the running itself and the self-discipline it requires. You feel that you are in control of your own body, and therefore not a victim, but a victor in your world."

Wow!

I hadn't thought of it that way, but Coach was right. Cross country was the one place where I felt I had some kind of influence over my destiny. I felt my best when I was running. I wanted to be a victor, not a victim.

We piled into cars to head to Old Humphrey. I rode shotgun in Coach Rusk's car, with Ferdy and Rory in the back seat.

Ferdy was rocking to his iPod, so Rory aimed his mouth forward.

"Coach, can I run today? Huh? Huh? I've been practicing real hard. I'm ready to run. Can I run? Huh?"

"Wait until we get there," Coach told him with a smile.

"Hey, Corey. Your name is Corey, right, but some of them call you Zip, right? You must be in the other homeroom. You're in sixth grade like me, right?"

I gritted my teeth. "No, I'm in eighth grade."

"Gee, you're little for eighth grade. You must be smart to get there ahead of me. Must be hard, huh, to hang out with all those big kids. Hey, Corey and Rory. We could be, like, a rock band or something, couldn't we? Corey and Rory in the rock band, Glory. Hey, neato bandito."

I thought it sounded like something on the Cartoon Network.

"But they call you Zip, huh? Funny name. Why do they call you Zip?"

"Because I run fast."

"Fast, huh. I run fast, too. I do everything fast."

Including talk, I thought.

Coach was grinning, enjoying this.

"I'll run with you, Corey, that's what I'll do, run with you, because I'm fast."

"Rory, could you quiet down. I need time to think."

"Think, huh? I don't need time to think."

"Shut up!"

"Oh, that's what you mean." He swiveled his mouth toward Ferdy. "You have an iPod, huh? An old one, antique even, but it still works, I guess. What are you listening to, Ferdy, what is it, huh?"

Ferdy ignored him. Ferdy was the exact opposite of this new kid: tall, quiet, deliberate, and not easily upset.

Rory grabbed the earphones off Ferdy's head, putting them up to one ear.

"Hey," yelled Ferdy, "give that back!"

"This is an iPod Classic, isn't it? I don't have one of these.

I collect them, you know, old iPods. I have eleven of them now.”

“Give it back.”

“Rock music, huh? Neato bandito. But I don’t know this band. ‘I want you to want me, I need you to need me…’ I like it. Who is it?”

“Cheap Trick. Give it back.”

“What do you want for it, huh? I’ll buy it from you.”

“Not for a million dollars. Give it back.”

Finally, Coach spoke up firmly. “Rory, give Ferdy back the iPod. And be quiet, please.”

He did, and he was, but by the time we pulled into Old Humphrey he looked like a balloon ready to pop. His parents were there waiting for him. I imagine they had enjoyed a nice quiet ride together.

The first thing Coach said was. “Stay away from the apples.” Last year’s runners got the joke, but the new ones were just confused. They looked up at the pretty red fruit like the humpbacked preacher from Texas pictured Eve looking at the tree in the Garden of Eden.

“All the runners new to the team get to run today.” A cheer went up from the newbies, while we oldies sat quiet on the grass. “I want the new runners to get their feet wet.”

Rory raised his hand. “Do we have to run through a creek or something?”

“No. I mean, I want you to get broken in.”

Rory raised his hand again, but Coach Rusk ignored him.

“Ferdy, Tyler, and Sally, who has a cold, will be sitting out today’s race. Betty Jean and Corey will run because they sat out here last year. Besides, Corey deserves the honor as the conference meet champion last year.” Rory looked at me with wonder. Yeesh. I hoped he didn’t want to be my BFF.

At the starting line, Old Humphrey’s team put their hands together and yelled, “Go, Humps!” We yelled, “Go,

Hamsters!" What a matchup.

I decided to run jackrabbit and see if I could get far enough ahead to hold out until the finish. Rory did keep up with me for a little while before he slacked off. Shelly was the one who stayed with me the longest, with Chad and two of the Humps maybe twenty feet back. The track was mostly woods, a lot like Butterworth, crooked and hilly.

The second referee was stationed near the apple trees, probably to prevent an apple attack like last year. After the next curve, Shelly puffed, "See you later. Good luck." When she dropped back, I ran alone under the dark shade and soft needles of a pine grove, before on a low hard packed spot I could hear the thump, thump of heavy feet right behind me.

With a grunt, Chad pulled even. He licked his lips, sneered "hasenpfeffer," and, as we rounded a corner, out of sight of everyone else, he delivered an elbow to my ribs sending me into a tangle of goldenrod.

"Told you I'd beat you, Zippo!"

By the time I recovered, one of the Humps got past me. Chad finished first, I came in third, and our team won. I should have felt better about that than I did.

The ride home was wonderfully quiet without Rory. Coach said, "Good job, Corey." That's all. He seemed to know when I preferred not to talk. Ferdy was alone with his iPod. When we parted at the school, Ferdy said, "Tomorrow at three?"

"Yeah, sure, see you then."

ooo

Nobody was home when I arrived. They didn't get home until supper time, Mom lugging a bag and a bucket of KFC, Dad carrying a new, pink Big Wheel Racer, and Sis hauling an armload of Annie. As we dug into extra crispy, mashed potatoes with gravy, and baked beans, I said, "I have good news."

"So do we," Sis exclaimed.

She was about to burst with it, so I got mine in fast. "We won our first meet at Old Humphrey."

Dad said, "Weren't they going to rename that place just plain Humphrey?"

Mom answered, "They had a town meeting. They couldn't agree whether it would be in honor of Hubert Humphrey or Humphrey Bogart, so they tabled the issue."

I repeated, "We won our first cross country meet, and I came in third place."

Mom said, "That's nice, honey."

Dad said, "Not first this time. But third is good, too."

Sis burst. "Now it's my turn. We're adopting!"

"What? Annie?"

"Both of them. We are going to adopt Annie and Kitty."

"You can do that?"

Mom explained, "Kitty's getting better now, but she doesn't have any family to help her. So, we made a decision."

"We had a family meeting, Corey," Dad added.

"Without me?"

Sis gushed, "We didn't need you. Three is a majority. We voted to adopt Kitty and Annie into our family."

Mom said, "Unofficially, of course. They need us. It's the right thing to do."

"But we don't have enough room," I said.

"Oh, they'll still live in their little trailer. We'll just help with Annie and food and all."

Dad said, "Your mother will go back to work full-time at Belle's so we can afford it, and we'll change our fostering to school-aged children so she can work the daytime shift."

I guess it's okay. I just wish they'd invited me to the meeting.

17

RASCALITY

Hu's invitation to Sunday dinner included going with him and his parents to Sunday morning church, which meant missing Zilch church in front of the TV. Last week, the humpbacked preacher from Texas fought off the devil with a whip and a chair. The head pastor at Grace Baptist Church, not Coach Rusk, preached without a whip, only a Bible. He talked about Jesus as if they were best friends.

Though this wasn't my family, I liked sitting with a family in church. Sarah waved to me from the other side where she sat with her mother and sister. That was a good sign.

My mouth was watering for some of that Kung Pao chicken at Hu's house. A big electric wok was steaming in the center of the table. Hu's mom brought out plates, chopsticks (silverware for me), sesame sticks, salad, and hot tea. Hu's father said grace in both Chinese and English.

Earlier in church, his parents surprised me by wearing American clothes and singing in English. Now they surprised me again. His mother lifted the lid from the wok, put two scoops on a plate, and set it before me, saying, "Nice American boy, good American food."

Beef stew.

After dinner, we played Chinese checkers. Don't play checkers, or any other game with Hu, by the way, if you want to win.

"Chinese checkers is not really checkers," Hu explained, "plus it isn't Chinese. The Germans invented it, but Chinese people like to play it. Like checkers, you jump over the other person's pieces, and your own, too, but they all stay on the board until they get 'home.' They are marbles, actually. Never mind. I'll show you while we play."

Fun game.

While we played, Hu shared his latest idea about what happened to Booger Schmidt. "The toxic waste crew found Booger trapped in the goo. They wrapped him in plastic and took him to their lab to analyze him, and found out that because Booger ate the stuff, he had superpowers as a human stink bomb. The military picked him up as a threat to national security. They plan to use him as a secret weapon in the war against eco-terrorism."

"Possible," I responded, "unless he wipes out the good guys, too."

My dad came for me at two-thirty, took me home to change into running clothes, and delivered me to Butterworth. Ferdy was waiting. The two of us decided to do the high school track first, rest a while, and then do our trail. He tuned in his iPod, while I tuned out my troubles, and we had a comfortable cruise.

During the break, I asked Ferdy if I could hear his music.

"Sure," he said, "long as you give it back."

I put on the earphones.

"You've got me all wound up and ready to go."

I said, "I like that. Is this group all you have on here?"

"Pretty much. They're a 70's rock band called Cheap Trick. They're all old by now, but they still sing, kind of like the Rolling Stones.”

“If they’re so old, why do you like them so much?”

“It’s a long story, and it’s kind of private.”

“We’ve got time, and I promise not to tell.”

“Okay. Cheap Trick was my father’s favorite band. Once when he was in college, he followed them all over the country like a groupie. They even knew him by name. He bought this iPod when they first came out and filled it up with Cheap Trick music. My dad was in the Army after he and Mom got married and stayed in the reserves after I was born. When I was seven, after we started running every day together, he was called up to go to Iraq. He gave me his iPod and told me to keep it safe for him and to keep running every day until he got back.

“He didn’t come back alive, and I kept running. When I listen, I feel close to him, and when I hear Cheap Trick, I feel like he’s running beside me.”

Wow, I thought. *I can’t imagine not having a father. I can’t imagine having a mother like Noford. And I really can’t imagine having no family at all like Kitty.*

After our second run, before we parted, Ferdy asked, “Do you think your friends would mind if I sat with you guys at lunch tomorrow?”

“I don’t know why not. Try it and see.”

ooo

In Hanway Middle School you can’t go anywhere unless you pass the principal’s office. I certainly couldn’t get past.

“Zilch,” commanded Principal Farraday, “recall and restate rule one.”

“Yes, Sir. You taught me to Position Your Person for Perceptivity.”

“Right. You are now responsible to report your resultant revelations.”

111

"Yes, Sir. I have penetrated the perimeter and perceived the place."

Yeesh. I was stuck in the p's.

"Results?"

"Well, sir, I positioned myself to see the whole cafeteria, and the most unusual activity seems to be in the corner near the garbage cans. Perhaps the stink in that area prevents the honest students from being close enough to hear them hatch their plans."

The principal's eyes glowed with pleasure. "Aha, a rift in the rampart. I shall remonstrate and require the rogues to relinquish their roguery and rectify their rascality."

I didn't understand a bit of it, except that the Scuds were about to get a lecture.

Even Mr. Farraday seemed to realize he had gone overboard because he took a deep breath. "Zilch, you are ready for your next

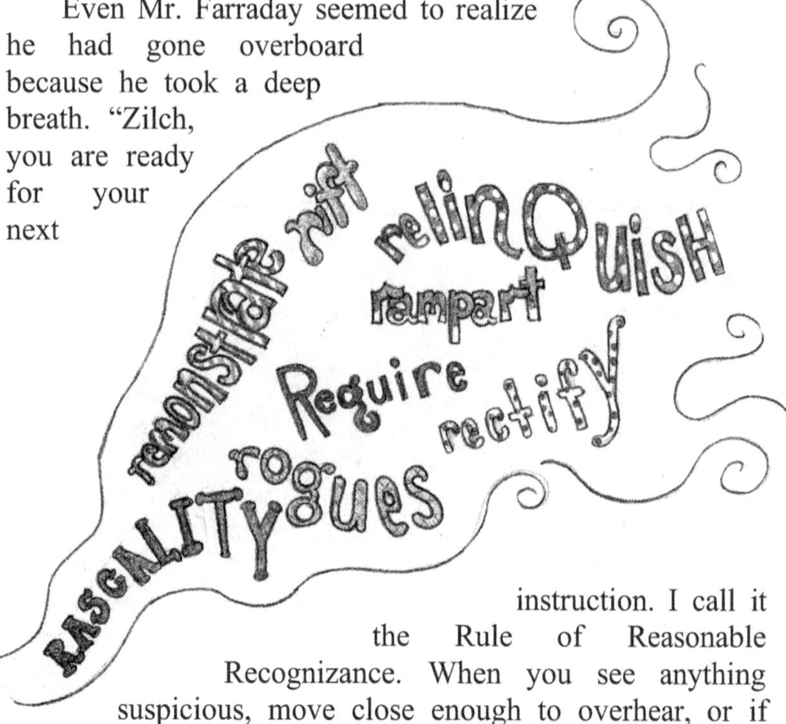

instruction. I call it the Rule of Reasonable Recognizance. When you see anything suspicious, move close enough to overhear, or if possible, even *inject* yourself into the situation in the role of a co-conspirator."

I think that made me what spies call a "mole," a counter spy, a double agent which would be easy, since I was doing it already.

When I reached the lunchroom I moled over to the Scuds table by the garbage cans. The atmosphere there was surprisingly fresh. I wasn't sure if it was the new trash bins or the absence of Booger.

Noford roared, "What're you doin' here, bug?" Then under his breath he muttered, "Whassup?"

"What's up is that if you don't want a lecture from Principal Farraday you'd better change your table."

As I stepped into the lunch line they invaded the opposite corner, ousting a clique of sixth-grade girls who took over the former Scuds table. As I collected my olive patty in guacamole sauce, our principal stomped in, waddled to the corner, and lashed the little girls with r-words they had never heard before. The girls fled in tears. I really felt guilty, but I hadn't told them to sit there.

When I reached the Buds table, Sarah asked, "What was that all about?"

"The Scuds didn't like something I said and moved."

"Boy, Corey, you're getting awfully brave."

"I have decided I don't want to be a victim anymore. I want to be a victor."

"Good for you!"

"As for Principal Farraday, I am afraid he may be losing his mind. He keeps grabbing me to tell me things in confidence that I can't repeat, and now he picks on those girls. You'll have to draw your own conclusions."

"I've thought he was nuts for a long time," Justine declared.

"Speaking of nuts," said Hu, "we have a new theory about

Booger. We think Noford decided to upgrade his friends. He tried to trade Booger for the Bosleys, but Booger put up such a stink that they got rid of him.”

“Got rid of him? How?”

“Maybe tied him up and put him on a train to California or a barge to New Orleans.”

Sarah told me, “You should ask since you aren’t afraid of the Scuds anymore. Go ask Noford. ‘Where’s your Booger?’”

I would do anything for Sarah, so I marched right up to Noford and asked, “Where’s your Booger?”

He stuck his fat finger up his fat nose and said, “Right—”

“No. Our school’s Booger. Where’s your pal Booger Schmidt?”

The whole room went suddenly still. Heads turned.

I let fly with it. “Where’s our Booger?!”

“What’s it to you, bug boy?”

“We miss him. The whole school misses him.” That was a stretch, but certainly everyone must have noticed the difference. I looked around the room and yelled. “Where’s our Booger?”

“Ain’t that sweet. But it’s none of your business.”

Someone nearby started it, and soon everybody joined in the chant, “Where’s our Booger? Where’s our Booger? Where’s our Booger?”

Being close, I could hear Amy speak in a little girl voice, “Make them stop, Nofie.”

Noford rose, lifted me up to his face, pulled me nose to nose, and roared. “Go away, bug. I ain’t gonna tell you nothin’ about Booger!”

No wink this time. He was serious. The chant stopped, and I went away.

As I left, I heard Amy say, in a normal voice, “Hey, guys, that gives me an idea.”

ALL THE NEWS

My father watches TV for the news, but every evening he reads the Hanway Herald for entertainment. That night he found the front page of the Hanway Herald so amusing that he passed it to me.
This is what it said:

ALL THE NEWS ABOUT THE OOZE

by H. H. Reporter Laura Fountain | A Hanway Herald Exclusive

The Ooze of Hanway, according to the Department of Inland Defense, was not a terrorist attack, nor an invasion from outer space, but a natural phenomenon. When asked for more detail, they denied the request, since that information is classified.

The Ooze video, recorded by a Hanway Middle School student on a smuggled-in iPhone, went viral last week. The Department of Inland Defense, in response, accused terrorists of attacking the Education Department's anti-obesity campaign, in an effort to cause all American children to be too overweight to serve in the military. The Ooze incident originated in the school cafeteria where the gourmet menu featured ceviche, a South American fish stew.

The more popular theory in Hanway was that intergalactic aliens had created the Ooze as a diversion while they kidnapped an exceptional Hanway student, whose name has not been released, for examination in their orbiting laboratory.

The DID news release yesterday rules out both theories, claiming that government laboratories analyzed the substance and found nothing but natural ingredients.

This paper's own reporters have interviewed several school employees. Principal Percival Q. Farraday refused to comment, except to say that the whole incident was "overblown."

One teacher, on condition of anonymity, described the harrowing experience. "I thought we all were going to die. The slime erupted from the trash bins like Mt. Vesuvius, spreading molten lava that pursued us, like a ravenous blob intent on consuming our tremulous flesh and acquiring our eternal souls to fill its own deficiency. I plan to write a book."

The official statement of the district school board termed it a "minor incident of little import," although they did close the school for a day and a half.

This reporter, on the following Monday, entered the school midday to find students lining the hallways, eating their lunch in an apparent sit-down strike, led by a student, one Noford Hammond, who was distributing food in the absence of school meals. Mr. Hammond deserves high praise for his charitable effort. When interviewed, he claimed he and the students were "just having a little fun."

The cafeteria staff seemed baffled. When questioned about what led up to the event, they called it a normal morning. A local fisherman had donated 100 pounds of Asian carp filets from the Sumac River, so the cooks used a government-approved gourmet recipe for seafood ceviche.

Some substitutions were made, since not all ingredients were readily available. With insufficient time to marinade the fish in lime juice, they boiled it in lemon extract and white vinegar with green food coloring. For fresh tomatoes they used five gallons of tomato juice, and in place of jalapeno peppers they added Uncle Henry's Flaming Hot Sauce. The head cook claims, "It came out just fine."

When questioned about the ceviche, student Justine Highcourt said, "Nobody actually ate the soup. We just dumped it in the trash cans."

William Hammer, the head custodian, when asked if he had noticed anybody or anything suspicious that morning said, "No, nothing out of the ordinary. I was only in the dining area for a few minutes. Principal Farraday had received complaints about a repugnant odor rising from the refuse repositories in the corner, but I took care of that. I put three open boxes of baking soda in each garbage bin."

The matter is unsolved as yet. However, the Department of Inland Defense assures the citizens of Hanway that the Ooze was "one hundred percent normal."

The residents of Hanway have serious doubts about that conclusion, and the school board is considering a lawsuit when they learn who is responsible for this disaster. The cost of the clean-up was exorbitant, and the insurance company refuses to cover it. Reportedly, the money will come from the athletic budget. When asked for more details, Principal Farrady said, "No comment."

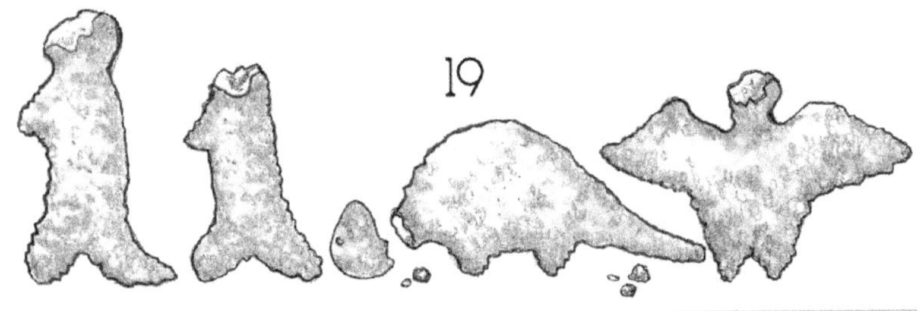

19

NOT GONNA HAPPEN

When I read the news article to my friends, Hu said, "Any science student could have told them not to do that."

"Not to do what?" asked Justine.

"Elementary, my dear Bud. Not to make garbage cans into volcanoes."

Speaking of volcanoes, Chad oozed over and erupted, "Geek, geek, geek, I eat geeks for lunch. What're you hatching now? A plan to shut down the school again?

Shelly spouted, "We'd rather shut you up."

"Not gonna happen. Got a message for you. We're taking over your table, so you might as well move before Noford comes in."

Shelly pronounced, "Nope. Not gonna happen."

I stood and said, "Nope."

The others got up and told him, "Not gonna happen."

Ferdy, who had just started eating lunch with us that week, was the only one who was tall enough to look Chad in the eye. He stepped over, got nose to nose with him, and said, "Nope."

The earth shifted, and Noford oozed over like a mud slide

through California. He grunted, "Get away from my table. Go sit with the garbage where ya belong."

"Nope," we all said together.

The Scuds formed a battle line. Chad poked his finger into Ferdy's chest and snarled, "This bean pole thinks he can take me. Let's do it."

Just then Coach Haggerty, who had drawn the short straw as lunch monitor that day, sauntered over. "What's going on, guys?"

Noford and the Bosleys were on the middle-school football team, and wanted to stay on it, I guess. Noford said, "Nothin', Coach. Just a huddle, that's all."

As the Scuds turned back toward the garbage cans, Chad stuck his finger in Ferdy's chest again and whispered, "Later."

We all thanked Ferdy for sticking up for us, but he just told us, "You can't give a bully what he wants. My dad taught me that."

ooo

When I came home after practice, I found my dad, little Annie, and even my sister, in orange t-shirts. I changed into mine, and away we went. Annie was pedaling furiously on her pink Big Wheel, with Sis pushing lightly from behind, laughing all the way. The girls turned back at the end of the block while Dad and I ran on through the neighborhood. When we reached our bus stop bench, I asked, "Dad, how do you deal with bullies?"

He answered, "You first have to judge whether you can beat them or not, then either face them down or back off. But there's one thing you never do."

"What's that?"

"You never give them what they want."

"How do you know what they want?"

120

"Son, all bullies want one thing. They may say other things, but what they want is for you to cower in fear. You can't give them that. They want to control you, to own you. What they really want is your soul. You can't give them what they want."

"That's weird, Dad. I heard the same thing already today."

"Oh, yeah? From your coach, I suppose. My basketball coach in high school said that all the time."

"No. A friend of mine said it. Ferdy Phillips."

"Phillips, huh? One of my teammates, Greg, had that last name. Great guy, power forward, tall, slim but strong. Nobody could intimidate him. Too bad he got killed in the war."

"Dad, Ferdy's father got killed in Iraq."

"How about that, Greg Phillips had a kid."

"Ferdy's a good guy, too. He doesn't talk much."

"Just like his dad."

"I guess so."

Dinner was ready a little early, chicken nuggets. Annie's were shaped like little dinosaurs. She growled and bit their heads off. Mine were just chunks I bit in half. Sis picked off the coating and ate the chicken inside. Dad popped them in his mouth whole.

Mom took a nibble, then said, "I'm going to the, uh, medical facility this evening to arrange for a certain person's release on Saturday."

Sis blurted, "Annie's mother ..." then clamped her hands over her mouth.

Annie had lined up her headless dinosaurs for extinction. She looked up and said, "My mother's name is Katrina Dagle, my name is Her-, Her-, Annie. We live at four-fourteen Leafy Lane in Hanway. Mommy makes me say that every day." She smiled, proud of herself, then giggled, "Mommy's real name is Kitty, like a kitty cat. I can't have a kitty cat, so I have a kitty mommy!" Then she proceeded to demolish her row of

Tyrannosaurus Rex.

Mom informed us that the "event" would be Saturday.

Once again, I would be left out. I said, "Our first home cross country meet is at Butterworth Park this Saturday. I was hoping you all could come and watch."

Mom said, "I'm sorry, Corey, but it will take us all day to get her settled, buy her groceries, get her prescriptions filled and all."

Dad added, "We promise to come to the next home meet if we possibly can."

Sis said, "I'm not making any promises."

"It's okay," I muttered, "I'm used to it."

"We're changing our foster care arrangement with DCFS," Mom explained. "We are asking for school age children now. The money isn't enough, and the state is so far behind on paying its bills that all we have is IOUs, so I'm going back full time at Belle's. I'll count on the two of you to get our foster children off to school in the mornings. I will go in early so I can be home by the time school lets out."

Sis was happy about it. "Does that mean I can pick out the clothes the little girls wear and dress them?" Mom nodded.

I was not so happy. The last thing I wanted to do was dress a six-year-old boy. With my luck we would get a miniature version of Rory Jones.

20

WHERE'S MY BOOGER

On Friday, the Scuds opened a new enterprise on the table by the garbage cans. Location, location, location. At Hanway School everyone had to go to that corner to dispose of their uneaten lunch. The Scuds table was piled high with t-shirts, at ten dollars a pop. The Scuds left their black leather jackets in their lockers and were wearing their wares.

Booger Schmidt in all his glory imprinted on t-shirts, who'da thunk it. I couldn't believe anybody had ever taken a picture of him, but there he was. Underneath his grimy face in big, block letters it said, "WHERE'S MY BOOGER?" On the back of the shirt it said, "WE WANT OUR BOOGER BACK!"

They were selling like, well, candy. And t-shirts aren't illegal, so they were selling in the wide open. In the spirit of reasonable recognizance, I walked over and asked, "Where did you get the shirts?"

Amy answered me. "My father owns a t-shirt shop."
"Oh. Where did you get that picture?"
"Nofie had one on his phone."
"Oh. What did Noford do to Booger?"
"None of your business."
Rumors flew again.

Booger was under quarantine as the bearer of six deadly diseases, and they were using his blood to make antitoxins. Hu's newest theory.

Booger's mother sold him for a six-pack of beer (Justine).

Booger had taken a shower, and because he was completely composed of dirt he had dissolved (Sarah).

The other Hanway kids must get more spending money than I do. By the end of lunch hour only one shirt was left, in triple-x size. I stopped at Principal Farraday's office to report the remarkable results of my reasonable recognizance. He went to the cafeteria to buy the last shirt.

ꙮ

Pennington rode in a purple bus, with purple horses on the side, wore purple uniforms with "Purple Ponies" stenciled on the back, and their fans drove behind them honking. Cross country is big stuff in Pennington, because there isn't much else. Their team must have a large budget, unlike ours. We don't have uniforms or a bus. Pennington always has a good cross country team. Hanway has a great coach and good runners, but a rag-tag appearance. We were embarrassed to be seen with them on the same trail.

Our Butterworth course, however, was much improved. Several parents, led by Betty Jean's biker dad, worked on it over last weekend, cutting brush, digging out rocks, and laying down pickup loads of some kind of ground-up tree bark and pine needle mulch.

Ferdy, Betty Jean, and Tyler got to run, while I sat out. My parents, if they had come, wouldn't have seen me run anyway. Besides, fans can only see the start and finish at Butterworth. The only way to see what's out in the woods is to run through it. The two referees just started the race and walked over to the water cooler to wait for the finish.

I broke up loose sticks to make a pile while I thought about the Scuds. They seemed to want to fight us, the Buds, as if we were a threat to them, and even though it was our six to their five, look at our six. Then look at their five.

The first runner out of the woods was Chad, with an evil smirk. Second was a Pennington horse, loping with a slight limp. Ferdy came out behind them, holding his side like he had a cramp, followed by a mixed clump of runners. When the places were all sorted out, Pennington won the meet by four points. The horse who finished second was crying "foul." I figured Chad had got him, but he pointed to Ferdy.

"He tripped me!"

When questioned, Ferdy, in obvious pain, said, "I fell. He tripped over me."

"But I was about to pass them both. They did it on purpose."

The judges conferred and then stated, "We cannot call a foul on hearsay. The results stand. Just be more careful next time."

Chad was soaking up the glory, two wins in a row for him. Shelly and I jogged over to Ferdy to ask what happened.

He gasped. "Chad ... elbow ... ribs."

"I knew it," Shelly said.

ooo

Again, I beat my family home, ran a few blocks through the neighborhood to stay in shape, showered, and watched the Cubs beat the Cardinals.

Around six, my family dragged in sad faced, carrying bags of burgers and fries. Sis took an envelope of fries to her room and shut the door.

"Is something wrong?" I asked.

"Your sister misses Annie already," Mom answered. "We all do."

"Did everything go okay?"

"Yes. We really should be happy for Kitty and Annie being back together, and we'll be seeing a lot of them, but somehow the house is going to feel empty."

I could feel it, too. I hadn't played with Annie or snuck her into bed with me when she asked for water in the middle of the night, like Sis did, but she did brighten the house up, a lot. The thought of it made me want to see A-lo again.

Maybe the next foster kid would be a little brother for me to pal around with, a kid who could learn cross country from me.

ooo

JV Youth Group with Sarah and Hu that Sunday night cheered me up a bit. I wondered if I should tell Coach about Chad, but he was busy with other kids. Sarah, Hu, and I sat on the church lawn, waiting for Sarah's sister to get out of the Senior High Youth Group.

126

I asked Hu, "Could you do me a favor? You have internet at the restaurant. Could you look up something for me?"

"No, I can't. My father won't let me use it for anything but business."

That I understood. My dad wouldn't allow a computer or cell phone in the house. He said, "The government records everything. It would be like inviting a spy into your home."

He didn't know he already had one.

Sarah spoke up, "I can do it. I have internet on my computer." That reminded me of how little I knew about Sarah's family life, except that her parents didn't get along. She didn't talk much about herself, and she wouldn't let me read her poetry.

"Thanks," I said. "Look up Greg Phillips, Ferdy's father. He was killed in Iraq when Ferdy was seven. My father says they played on the same Hanway basketball team."

"Okay. Yes. I remember him dying, but I was just a kid. I'll look it up."

"There's something else we ought to talk about."

"What's that?" Hu asked.

"What should we do about the Scuds?"

PART III: THE IDES OF MARCH

You don't have to read this, but you should.

Sarah was reading Shakespeare's *Julius Caesar* aloud. I couldn't make sense of some of it, but I knew I never wanted to hear her say "et tu, Brute" to me. So I found in the library a book about him to get the real story.

Julius Caesar is one of the greatest men in the history of the world. A brilliant military leader, like Napoleon, he expanded the Roman Empire by winning wars in France, England, Spain and across Europe and parts of Africa and Asia, until Rome ruled major parts of the world. He made history, wrote history, reformed and reorganized his world, built roads and cities and libraries, replaced dishonest governors, and even came up with our present-day calendar (think "July"). He laid the way for his adopted son, Caesar Augustus, to start the Pax

128

Romana. No, that's not a disease like chicken pox. It means the Roman Peace, which lasted 200 years. As long as you did what they told you to do you had peace. If you didn't, they crucified you. His name became the title of the emperors after him, plus Russian Czars and German Kaisers.

What was his reward for all this? He got stabbed in the back, literally, on the Ides of March, in his own hometown.

I know how that feels.

21

LOST AND FOUND

Julius Caesar had his Ides of March; I had my Ides of October.

All I can say is, when things at last seem to be going your way, watch out. For two weeks things were quiet. Sure, things were happening, but they were not happening to me. I didn't even have a cross country meet. The Scuds were preoccupied with their booming business. Nearly the whole school was covered with Boogers.

Even we, the Buds, bought them. A lot of kids wore them every day. The boys never washed theirs, so soon they exuded (Sarah's word) the spirit of Booger Schmidt. The girl's decorated their shirts with flower decals and doused them with perfume in protest.

Principal Farraday was preoccupied, too, with trying to stop it all. He wore his 3x shirt to the next school board meeting, and the board voted to make them illegal. The next morning the following headline was on the front page of the *Hanway Herald*: WHERE'S MY BOOGER?

The feature article, by Laura Fountain, under a smiling Noford Hammond wearing a huge Booger shirt, said:

Public-spirited students at Hanway Middle School have mounted a campaign on behalf of a missing student, one Booger Schmidt, who disappeared around the time of the Ooze, by distributing t-shirts with his likeness. City police have taken notice, having found the boy's mobile home in Shady Lane Estates abandoned and in shambles. The authorities are treating it as an active crime scene.

Eighth grader Justine Highcourt commiserates that "school is just not the same without our Booger." Principal Farraday could not be reached for comment. Since the School Board was in session during the writing of this article, it is assumed they are concerned for this child's safety, as well.

The campaign is being led by Noford Hammond, who seems to be the de facto leader of the student body. Mr. Hammond calls Mr. Schmidt "my very best friend."

This paper commends the Hanway School system for their compassionate sponsorship of this movement. Should any citizens wish to join the campaign, the t-shirts are now available at Too-a-Tee in downtown Hanway.

Should you have information pertinent to the investigation, please phone the Hanway Police Department or the Hanway Herald.

The school board backed off their ban, so Booger shirts quickly became legal again until that Friday, when the FBI, without warning or explanation, herded the girls into the dining hall and the boys into the gymnasium. One Bosley went in each direction, but I don't know which one went where.

They confiscated all our Booger shirts, replacing them with white ones which should have said FBI, but said nothing. All the shirts were extra-large. Mine hung to my knees, but Noford's barely reached his belly button. Some of the girls were really, really embarrassed.

So, the Feds do have Booger, we concluded, and they don't want a big thing made of it. The opposite is what happened. New rumors flew, like migrating geese, too many to count.

By the next Monday the Scuds were back in business, selling Booger Bands—head bands and wrist bands that said, "GIVE US OUR BOOGER BACK!"

Meanwhile the Buds had peace.

Hu, who always seemed to be thinking, opened our conversation with, "As I see it, we have four choices how to handle it if the Scuds decide they want to face us down again. Our animal instincts give us two—fight or flight—and our human intelligence hands us two more—reason or compromise."

We looked at him like, what language are you speaking?

He adjusted and continued, "Let's take them one at a time. We would have an advantage in the flight thing, since four of you run cross country and I run home every day. We could outrun them, except for Chad. He would catch one of us."

"Excuse me!" Sarah squawked. "That would be me he would catch."

"Can't you run?" asked Shelly.

"Corey says I run like a girl."

Shelly and Justine glared at me.

"Well, she does."

Hu said, "We all pledged to be loyal and true, so that rules out flight. The problem is that with the fight reflex the Scuds have a slight advantage."

"Slight?" Justine said. "I'd call it a big fat advantage."

"I could take on Chad or Noford," declared Ferdy, "but what about the rest of you?"

"I'd take on the one you didn't, Ferdy," Hu asserted. "What about you, Shelly?"

"I've got Amy."

Justine chimed in, "I'd take Tori, if I can figure out which one she is."

Sarah looked at me. I confessed, "I've been beaten up a couple of times, but I've never been in a real fight in my life."

"Me neither," she said. "Let's try another way."

Hu suggested, "Maybe we could reason with them, talk them out of hurting us."

Justine responded, "Good luck with that."

"Or maybe we could compromise."

"The trouble with compromise," Ferdy said, "is that nobody ends up happy, plus, to get compromise, both sides have to have something to offer. What do we have to offer the Scuds?"

That was more than Ferdy usually said, and smarter than I expected. The bell for class time rang before we could talk it out.

ⱺⱺⱺ

Normal at home was Mom cooking good food again, our family talk around the table without worrying about what little ears would hear, and Sis watching Dr. Phil instead of Sponge Bob, but normal didn't feel as good as it used to feel.

One time Annie came over for the night so Kitty could rest. For some reason all Annie could talk about was fire trucks and police cars.

The next evening when Dad plunked into his recliner with the Herald, he announced, "This must be what Annie was talking about. An abandoned trailer burned up in Shady Lane Estates. No casualties, but quite a blaze."

He turned a page. "Here's another one. The Rest Stop Robbers struck again. That's six times now. A man and a woman catch people along the Interstates in the rest stop bathrooms, steal their purses, wallets, cell phones and car keys, and take off in one of the cars, leaving another stolen car behind. I sure hope they catch them soon."

Mom had an announcement of her own. "The social worker called. We'll be getting a boy next week, as soon as he

134

recovers from some kind of injuries."

Now I'll have a little brother, not as little as A-lo, but a boy I can have some fun with, teach some things. Maybe he'll look up to me like a big brother.

ooo

When I arrive at school each day, running from home, I use the side door, so I didn't see what the others saw. They were milling around in the hall, the roar of the jabbering drowning out even the homeroom bell. Sarah grabbed my hand and held it, which felt good, but she was pulling me out the front door to the school announcement sign. Girls were sitting around it crying. Somebody had painted across it in blood red:

ooo

Our next meet was at Whitmore. The Whippets were our poorest competition. Coach had Chad, Shelly, and Rory sit this one out.

Running felt good. I felt good. This was my day. We

started out running in a pack—Ferdy, Justine, Betty Jean, Tyler, and I. A long-legged Whippet with a long blonde ponytail ran close to me. When her hair blew in the wind, I got a face full.

Betty Jean and Tyler dropped back, but the other four of us ran close, Ferdy in the lead.

"Pass?" asked Justine.

"Pass," I answered.

Ferdy gave thumbs up. I could hear him singing in rhythm with his feet:

Don't just sit there with your head in your hands

He paused for a deep breath.

Get up, get up, get on the ball.

Blondie went with us. As the three of us rounded the last corner, Justine said, "Kick?"

"Kick," I answered.

Her legs were longer, I could move mine faster. Blondie had no kick left. The two of us were neck and neck, but I had one more kick than her and won by a hair. Blondie finished third and Ferdy fourth. Our team won the meet easily.

Justine gasped, "I can beat you, Cory."

"I know you can."

"But I'll play fair."

"I know you will."

"Hey, guys, what are your names?" asked the blonde girl. "Mine is Gloria."

"Hi Gloria, I'm Justine, and this is Zip Zilch."

"I've heard about you," Gloria said.

Shelly was really glad to see us. Rory had been talking to her ever since Chad shoved him away. She and Rory ran over to congratulate us. Chad didn't.

Rory chirped, "That was fast, like, lightning fast. Wow, I'm gonna run that fast when I'm in eighth grade, too, I bet. I'll run even faster, I will."

When I got home, I announced, "I have big news, I won the race!"

Mom said, "That's nice dear. I have big news, too."

Dad said, looking up from the paper, "Good job, Son. I have big news, too."

Sis said, "I have no news at all."

Dad's big news was, "They caught them, the Rest Stop Robbers. The troopers were hiding in the bathroom stalls. They're home-grown criminals, Butch Roach from Sumac, and Greta Schmidt from Hanway. What a relief."

Mom's big news was, "We'll have our new foster boy on Monday. His name is Alvin."

Great, Alvin, a chipmunk. I hoped he wouldn't chatter like Rory.

All day Monday I was shaky. When the Buds asked why, I told them I was about to get a little brother.

"Don't get your hopes up, Corey," Sarah said.

I should have listened. After all, it was October 15, the ides. As soon as cross country practice ended I zipped home. Dad met me at the door.

"Is he here, Dad? Alvin?"

"Yes. He's in the bedroom."

I knocked at what used to be my door. A reedy voice called, "Come in."

I opened the door and met him face to face. His smell was different, but I could not mistake that face.

"Hi, Zip," he said.

A Scud had landed in my house.

22

ALVIN

I about choked on my tongue. "Boo ... Boo ... Booger?"

"Booger is gone. I'm Alvin."

Shock, I suppose. Hu would call it "catatonic." I stood there like a robot with a dead battery. My mind was picturing my first meeting with Booger and Noford at Weasel Creek. So much had changed since then that it felt like another life. But now I felt like I was hovering over the creek again, ready to splash.

"Earth to Zip! Are you there?"

"But ... but ... but ..."

"Kind of surprised, huh?"

"But ... you are dead."

"No. Booger is dead."

"Did you paint that on the sign board at school?"

"No, but the social worker told me about it."

"Did Noford?"

"No, but I know who did."

"Who?"

"Butch."

"Who is Butch?"

"You don't get around much, do you? Don't you watch the news?"

"Nope."

"Don't you read the newspaper?"

"Only when my dad shows me something."

"Butch has been all over the news—Butch Roach, the Rest Stop Robber. He wrote that stuff on the sign 'cause he was braggin' 'bout killin'' me."

"Why would he do that?"

"Zip, you sure are a dull knife. He wanted to kill me, and he thought he did kill me, because I'm a witness, of course. Don't you pay attention at all? The other Rest Stop Robber's name is Greta Schmidt."

"Oh."

"He beat me up and said he'd kill me if I told on him."

"So, where have you been the last month?"

"Hiding from Butch."

"Where?"

"Look, Zip. Some things I can tell you, and some I can't. Since I'm a witness, the FBI made it clear that I have to keep some things secret from you, and you have to keep secret what I do tell you. Do you understand?"

Secrets I did understand. God knows I had been keeping a bunch of my own lately. I said, "Yeah, I'll keep your secrets, pinky swear."

"I can tell you some things about me, but I can't talk much about Butch and Greta."

"Okay. So where have you been hiding?"

"In Noford's attic."

"Did Noford know?"

"Of course. He put me there, but his dad didn't know at first. Noford brought me food and water and puzzle books and day-old newspapers, and stuff. It was better than home."

"I'm confused."

"Yeah, I noticed."

"You seem sort of, like, well, a normal person. Not like Booger Schmidt."

"Bingo. Booger Schmidt is dead. I'm Alvin now. I never was Booger at all. He was just an act I put on for show."

"An act? You didn't smell like an act."

"Yeah, that part was real. The trailer didn't have water or electric, no money to pay the bills, no way to wash up or wash clothes. Beer was the only drink in the house. I had to go to the creek out back for a bath or a drink. No food either. Mom got food and a shower when men fed her and took her to a motel. I didn't."

"How did you stay alive?'

"You learn. You manage. Noford snuck me food and soda. His Pop would bring groceries sometimes, and I would hide some before Greta took it to trade for beer. But the Booger thing was an act to keep people from finding out about me."

"Noford knew."

"Yeah. He's the only friend I ever had, so I played Booger with him. Booger made him look smarter and meaner, too."

"But you are a normal person. For real?"

"No. I don't think I'll ever be normal, but I can be different. You thought I was stupid, didn't you."

"I suppose so. Another thing, this Greta person is your mother?"

"Yeah."

"Why do you call her Greta, not Mom?"

"Long story. When I was little, if I would say mama or mommy or mom, she would smack me in the face and yell, 'You call me Greta, you bastard boy.' She never called me Alvin, just called me that."

"Ouch."

"Yeah, ouch. She'd say, 'If I'd had any money, I'd a got ridda you, you know, and you wouldn't be nothin' at all."

"Double ouch. Why are you telling me all this stuff?"

"The police doctor told me I should talk about it, so I could put it behind me."

"Why tell it to me?"

"Who else? You're here, aren't you? Besides, you are the only person except for Noford and his Pop who ever treated me with respect."

I must have looked puzzled, because he said, "You don't remember it, do you. Last year, when Noford's Pop was in jail, you sat down next to me like I was a real person. You listened to me, and you helped Noford. I never forgot that."

"Yeesh, Booger, I'm sure sorry you got such a raw deal."

"Zip, don't call me Booger, okay. Booger's dead. Call me Alvin."

"Okay, Alvin. Call me Corey."

"I'm really tired, Corey. We can talk more another time."

"Yeah, okay, but you should know that on TV Alvin is a chipmunk. You need a nickname. Can I call you Al?"

"All right. I can be Al."

23

VINNY

Next morning, Booger—I mean Alvin—I mean Al—was in the shower all morning. Not really, but it seemed that way. After twenty minutes of waiting, Sis yelled down the stairs to me, "Can I use the shower down there?"

I can brush my teeth, wash my face and comb my hair in three minutes, so I was done with it. I yelled back, "Sure you can. Look out for the mousetraps." She *ooo, ick, ugh, yucked* all the way down on her tip toes. I got dressed in my dungeon cell and went upstairs. The FBI banged on the front door, four of them. I opened it, they came in, stood outside the bathroom door waiting for Alvin to finish, then got him dressed to go.

Sis came up wrapped in a beach towel, screamed, and ran back down. Snap. "Ow!"

Once the FBI hustled Booger—Alvin—Al—into their black Tahoe, I yelled in the basement doorway, "All clear."

Sis hopped back up, glaring at me for some reason. "The Feds got him for wasting water, I'll bet. Going to keep him in custody from now on, I hope. Why was he in there so long?"

"Making up for hundreds of showers missed, I think."

"What was the FBI—never mind. I don't want to know."

142

Mom and Dad were long gone to work. I didn't need to get Al off to school. So, I grabbed my backpack and a granola bar, locked the door, and jogged away to my daily fate.

Bursting with news I was not allowed to tell, I approached the Buds table not knowing what to say. They were all there but Ferdy.

Sarah spoke first. "I did what you asked, Corey, looked up Greg Phillips. I should say Sergeant Gregory Ferdinand Phillips. Guess what?"

"What?"

"Ferdy's father is a genuine hero, purple heart, silver star, *everything*. The story was front page in the Herald, picked up by USA Today and even Newsweek, with his picture in uniform. He was gorgeous, girls. Maybe you should get to know Ferdy better."

Justine said, "I know him quite well, thank you. Or I did. We shared a crib at times when we were babies." Her eyes went up to the side like she was digging up old treasures in her mind. "Ferdy's dad was my dad's best friend. They were at my house all the time. Harley and Ferdy and I played tag, and hide and seek, and Candyland all the time. That ended when I was seven. My dad wouldn't talk about it, so I never knew why."

I asked Sarah, "What happened to him."

She had printed out a copy and handed it to me. "His platoon was leading a convoy of food supplies to the army base outside Baghdad. He was in the lead Jeep when they hit an IUD that flipped the Jeep over, killing the driver and breaking Ferdy's father's back. He dragged himself behind the wreck, found his weapon, propped himself up behind a wheel, and held off a band of terrorists climbing over a wall while the rest of the soldiers escaped. He bled to death before reinforcements got back to him."

"That's amazing."

"Yes. It made me cry.

"What made you cry," Ferdy said, coming up behind us as we bent over the news story.

"What your father did," Sarah answered.

His faced turned red. He said, "I cry every morning when I wake up."

"We're sorry, Ferdy," said Shelly. "We didn't know."

"Don't be sorry. I'm not. He did what was right and saved soldiers' lives, and I'm proud of him. I just miss him."

Noford and the Bosleys slinked past. Noford croaked, "Golly gee, gosh whiz, look at all the sad face geeks."

I wanted to clobber him, but it wouldn't have been the right thing to do.

On the way to class, Principal Farraday got me again, right in front of everybody, and pulled me into his torture chamber.

"Zilch, you are remiss in your responsibilities. Reasonable recognizance requires results."

"Sir, I haven't seen anything to report. They don't seem to be selling candy anymore. Maybe you scared them away."

"Ridiculous! Wrongdoing is rife. They cannot refrain."

"I'll look harder, Sir, but you should know 'wrongdoing' starts with a 'w.'"

He looked sideways at me like he was surprised I could spell. "Be relentless, Zilch. Pursue righteous refutation of wrong, like that Hammond boy."

I almost choked, but managed to cough out, "I'll try."

When Noford pulled me into the boys room, all I could tell him was, "Principal Farraday has his eye on you."

That day the Scuds had a half-price sale on the Booger Bands, since Noford knew the school was about to get our Booger back in Alvin form. They'd be looking for another business. You had to give them credit; they never seemed to run out of ideas.

Booger was back, as Alvin, when I got home that day. Dad had bought him an orange shirt like mine. We ran together, slowly, since Alvin, Al, didn't have much energy. I always knew he was skinny but didn't know he was almost starved. No wonder he always ate the school lunches. At supper that day he ate three bratwursts and a half plate of sauerkraut.

Supper was quiet. Sis seemed upset for no reason. Nobody knew what to talk about, so I thought I would break the silence.

"So, Boo, uh, Al, how long do you think you'll be staying here?"

Mom asked, "Boo? What does boo mean?"

Alvin bailed me out. "Just a middle school word, like 'bro' means about the same thing. And to answer your question, boo, I might just stay here forever."

That was the second time in my life I saw my sister choke on Jello.

"The food's great. I have my own room, with a nice warm bed, and you people are so nice to me, why should I leave?"

"That's good," Dad said. "You're welcome in our home as long as you need to be here."

I changed the subject. "So, boo, are you coming to school tomorrow?"

"Maybe, if the cops don't get me first."

That made my mother choke.

I tried to explain, "The FBI came for him this morning and took him away."

"What?"

"He didn't do anything wrong."

"No, I'm a witness, a survivor. They've been asking me questions about things I know, but I can't tell. Didn't DCFS dump any crap on you about me?"

"We don't use that word in this house, Alvin," Mom said.

"Oh, sorry. Could I have a list?"

"We don't allow that kind of attitude either," Dad said. "We do have rules you will need to learn. For example, my daughter tells me, you were in the shower this morning for half an hour. From now on you have a five-minute limit."

He glared at my sister, but said, "Sorry."

Dad said, "All the social worker told us was that your house burned down, and your mother is in jail, and you are homeless."

"That's true, but it isn't all bad. Look at these new clothes they gave me, three sets. And you do have a nice shower, with soap and everything. That shampoo smells nice."

"You used my shampoo?" Sis yelled. She stomped to the bathroom, came out with an armload of her stuff, hauled it into her room, and slammed the door. Sis can be touchy at times.

After Al went into his room, Sis came out and whispered to Dad, "He's creepy. I want a lock on my door."

"Okay, honey. I'll go to Ace Hardware now."

I was in my cave doing homework when I heard the bolt slide and footsteps on the stairs.

He looked at the traps on the stairs and the D-con in the corners of my room. "Hey, mice, huh? I'm used to mice. Don't taste bad, with ketchup."

I gagged.

"Just kidding. I came to tell you I've changed my mind about my name. Alvin is a chipmunk, but Al can be just anybody, like the guy that sells cigarettes at the 7-11. I want to be called Vinny. A Vinny is a somebody."

"Okay, Boo, uh, Al, uh Vinny."

He laughed, "That's too long for a name. Just call me Vinny."

"You really look different, Vinny. Clean, hair combed, new clothes. Nobody at school will know who you are."

"That's the way I want it. I'll be the new kid, Vinny."

"Are you going to sit with Noford, like before."

"Yep. He's like my brother, you know."

"There are other kids sitting with him now."

"Yep, Noford told me. He said business is goin' good, sellin' Booger stuff, but he's gonna change that now that I'm comin' back, even if nobody knows it's me. Noford's got a new leather jacket for me."

"You aren't going to burn down my house, are you, like you burned the trailer."

"That wasn't me. Butch did that. I snuck back in the middle of the night to get my stuff, and Butch caught me. He was there with a gas can to burn up any evidence in the place. He beat me up, knocked me out and torched the place. Good thing I woke up. I had cut a trap door under the trailer so I could escape whenever Greta brought home some drunk for the night. I got out that way."

"Yeesh. No wonder he thought you were dead. He was bragging, wasn't he, when he wrote 'Booger is dead' on the school sign."

"Yeah. But he's a goner now. The Hanway cops, the state police, and the FBI are arguing about who gets him first. Uh-oh, I shouldn't a' told you that stuff. That might come up at trial, attempted murder, you know, and arson. Don't tell anyone, okay?"

"Okay, but why did you tell me?"

"I guess I think of us as two of kind, you know, with all the secrets we got to hide. I know yours, too, about being Farraday's snitch, and being, like, a double agent for Noford. Your friends don't know anything about it, do they? So, I figure if I keep your secrets, you'll have to keep mine, right? We're two of a kind."

Yeesh. Two of a kind with Booger, uh, Alvin, uh, Al, uh, Vinny Schmidt.

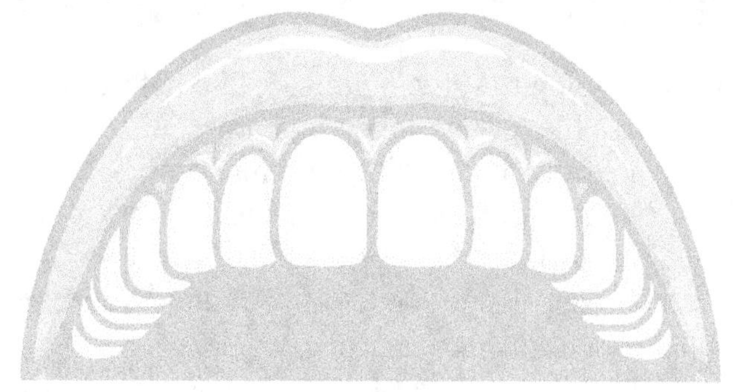

24

THE VINNY BUZZ

Vinny didn't do school on Wednesday. The social worker took him to the dentist—all day. He came home so numb he couldn't suck soup through a straw. Turns out, he had never been to a dentist before.

Vinny didn't do school on Thursday. They took him to a doctor to get shots. He had never been to a doctor before. They took him to the optometrist. He came home with glasses. He could see his food, but his arms were too sore to lift a spoon, and his face was too sore to chew.

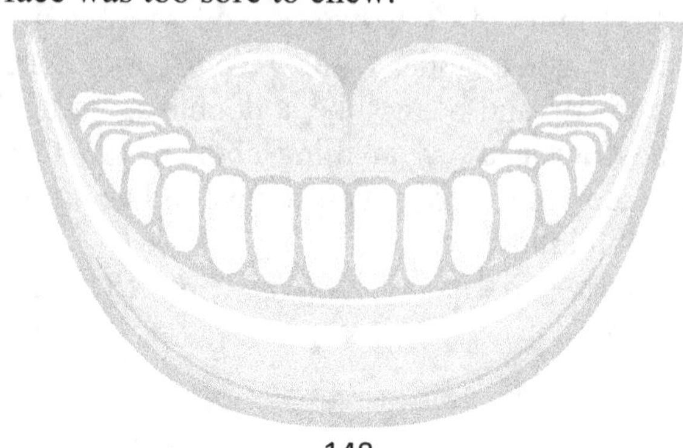

So, Friday was his first day of school. In homeroom the buzz was, "Who's that new kid sitting at Booger's desk?"

"Booger's dead, so I guess his desk was available."

"Spooky. I wouldn't want to sit in a dead kid's desk. They should burn it up."

"I wonder if he knows he's sitting in the desk of death."

"He's kind of cute" (girls).

"I could take him in a fight" (boys).

He was dressed in Dockers pants, Chaps shirt, top two buttons not buttoned, New Balance shoes, hair slicked back, sunglasses, and an attitude. The girls were more than curious, and the guys a bit afraid. When he sat by Noford at lunch he proved what kind of guy he was.

When the FBI came to the cafeteria to get him, the place went wild. Words like "witness protection," "mafia kid," "psycho killer," and "movie star hiding from his fans, trying to be normal" were circling like bees. Everyone was a-tingle except for me and the Scuds. In their distracted state, some kids even ate the squash quiche with fish balls.

"What's his name?"

"Vinny."

"Oooh, Vinny. Italian."

"Go talk to him when they bring him back."

"You talk to him."

"Who is he?" asked Sarah.

"No idea," said Hu.

"Fascinating," said Justine.

"Double trouble," muttered Shelly.

Ferdy turned to me. "Corey, you're the only one not saying anything. What do you know that we don't."

"I know who he is."

"Give."

"You have to figure that out for yourselves."

"What did he do?"

"I can't tell you."

"Hmmph!"

"Sworn to secrecy."

"You are lying. It's a trick. You don't know a thing."

After the buzz died down to a hum, Hu said, "Speaking of tricks, our youth group will be doing something fun for Halloween, and Pastor Rusk needs all the help he can get. Do you guys want to have some fun?"

"Sure," I said, "if you will tell us what it is."

I was thinking that if this is anything like last year's Pumpkin Party, it will be a hoot.

Hu explained, "Our church educational wing has sixteen classrooms, eight on each side of a long hallway, with the kids' worship center at the end. Each door will have a sign that says, '*Knock and say TRUST OR TREAT!*' Behind each door will be people in costume who will give each kid a choice. They can choose the treat they can see, or they can trust for something better and reach through a hole into a box for something they can't see."

Sarah added, "My sister and I plan to dress as clowns and give them a choice of a mini-Snickers bar or the secret box. If they choose to trust us, they'll pull out a big Snickers."

Hu said, "My mother and father will be dressed in their Chinese duds and give the kids a choice of a wrapped peppermint or reach in the box to pull out a Christian fortune cookie."

"You have Christian fortune cookies?" I asked.

"We give them out all the time in the restaurant. They're delicious. Inside they have a Bible verse on one side and a saying on the other, like 'Jesus will treat you to a better life.'"

Sarah said, "We need more people to take some doorways. There are seven left."

All the Buds agreed to do it, if their parents approved. Sarah squeezed my hand and said, "Ask your sister and her boyfriend Jimmy, would you?"

My first thought was that Sis might rather be flying past the moon on her broom that night, but it was nice having Sarah friendly and trusting again, so I agreed to ask.

ꝒꝒꝒ

My Dad had questions, of course. I had answers. They gave me permission.

I turned to my sister. "Sarah wonders if you and Jimmy would like to help."

"Oh, Sarah. You would do anything for Sarah, wouldn't you."

"Yes. Would you like to help?"

"Who will be there?"

"A lot of my friends, the middle school youth group, and some of the high school youth. Jimmy goes to that Youth Group sometimes. Ferdy and I will be doing one door."

"Okay." Sis said.

"What?"

"Okay. Jimmy will do whatever I tell him we're doing."

Weird, Sis wasn't usually so cooperative.

Mom said, "I have something for us to talk about, too. Kitty wants us to come to her place on Sunday at three. She wants you there, too, Corey. She says that she has something very important to discuss with us that involves us all. She wants to talk during Annie's nap time."

"What's it about?" Sis asked.

"I don't know, but she was insistent that all four of us should come. Not you, Alvin. Sorry. Do you have somewhere else you could go?"

He said, "I'll go over to my friend Noford's house. No problem."

"Is everybody on board, then?"

I said, "I usually run with Ferdy at three, but I'll tell him I can't this week."

"Good, I want you to meet Kitty. You will like her, for sure."

000

Later, Vinny came down the steps to my cave. "That was awesome!" he said.

"What was awesome?"

"Hearin' your family talk with each other like that. I never saw anything like that before."

"Really? We do it all the time."

"Wow. I guess the Feds yankin' me out of school musta made for a lot of talk there, too."

I laughed. "Oh, yeah. You are everything from the Vice President's love child to an Italian kid movie star, to a 20-year-old narc under cover."

"Hah! I ain't never been popular before. I like bein' Vinny. You didn't tell them?"

152

“Nope. Nothing to tell.”

“Noford made his other friends not tell, neither. Chad really wanted to. Noford threatened to take away his motorcycle jacket. This is more fun than I ever had in my whole life.”

“It is kind of fun to watch.”

“Ya know, Zip, you ain’t so bad. We could be friends, maybe. Noford and I want to see how long it takes before anybody figures out who I am.”

“Might be a long time.”

“Yep. It might.”

25

OUT OF THE FOG

Rain splashed down the next morning—not thunder and lightning, or the cross country meet at Fogerty would have been cancelled—just plain rain. Coach had me sit in the back with Ferdy and had Rory sit in front with him. Ferdy and I were glad that Coach took the brunt of the word-flood.

"Hey, I like riding shotgun. That must mean you like me, huh? I like you, too, and I like to talk to you, and this is great to talk to you on the way to... uh ...?"

"Fogtown."

"Frogtown. Funny name. I've never been to Frogtown, ever, in my whole life even. Where is Frogtown? Why do they call it Frogtown? Are there frogs there? I like frogs. I used to have a pet frog named Hopper, because he hopped, you know, and he was, like, green and ..."

"Not Frogtown, Fog-town. The real name is Fogerty, but people call it Fogtown because it's always foggy there. Today I want you to run so I can judge how ..."

"Foggy, huh, not froggy. Oops, that's funny. My mother says I'm funny, too, the way I always ..."

154

"... talk all the time," said Coach.

"Hey. How did you know what she says? Do you know my mother?"

"No, but I'm getting to know you. Rory, if you want people to like you, you need to learn to talk *with* them, not to them or at them."

"I talk with other kids all the time, but they don't say much. Sometimes they just walk away. That's kind of rude."

"Yes, well, maybe I can help with that. When you're with me, we'll have this secret signal, just between us. When I close my lips tight and put my finger in front of them, like this, pointing straight up, you stop talking right away. Okay?"

"That's funny. My father has the same signal. You do know my mother and father, don't you. My father says..."

Coach used the signal, and then repeated, "Okay?"

"Okay."

"That's better. Let me talk to you a minute, while you stay quiet. I've been watching you run, and you have real potential. You are naturally fast, but your technique is all wrong, and you have the disadvantage of being small. We'll work on how you run, so that when you grow, in a year or two, you can win some races. I worked hard with Corey last year and he ..."

The dam burst. "Yeah, Corey, huh? I want to run like Corey. They call him Zip. Did you know that? Zip means nothing, but I think he's something. Zip means fast, too, so they must call him Zip because he's fast, like he runs, like, in a zip. I want to run in a zip, too, so I can ..."

I was ready to yell from the back seat, *"Rory, zip it!"* But Coach gave the signal and Rory actually stopped. Maybe he could learn to shut up before someone choked him to death.

At that point I closed my ears to it because of the pain. The pain of hearing Rory was not as bad as the pain that I was being replaced by him as Coach Rusk's project. Now, who could I tell my troubles to? I tapped Ferdy on the shoulder and asked him what he was listening to. He took off his earphones and put them on my head.

...You can go where the music is loud ♫
And you won't be so lonely...

Ferdy plucked the earphones back off me. "That's a favorite one," he said.

I understood. "It's about being lonely."

"Yeah, it is. I went a long time without friends. Thanks for letting me into your gang."

I'd never thought of the Buds as a gang.

"Corey. I've never won a race. I've come close, but not won. You have. Could you teach me how to win?"

"Teach you how? Coach is better at that."

"Oh, he's helped me with how to run, but he says I still run like a robot. You, on the other hand, run with your gut, your feelings. So, maybe, you could teach me how to do that."

"Okay, I'll try. That reminds me I can't run with you in Butterworth tomorrow. Family plans."

ooo

The rain had let up and the sun was coming out when we plunged into the crater of fog called Fogerty. If a rainbow came out, you wouldn't see it. I wondered if the people in Fogtown had ever seen a rainbow.

Coach drove about ten miles an hour, searching for the school. When we found it in the swamp surrounding it, we discovered that Betty Jean's biker dad had raised a big tent, and her mom had a big container of hot chocolate ready. They had set up several camper chairs in the tent, too.

The Fogtown Frogs were in a tent nearby, with water, but

no chocolate. When Shelly's family drove in, all the girls on the other team ran over, hugged her, and began gabbing. Funny thing, though, not even one of the boys came over to talk with Chad, or even waved hello.

Coach told me I would sit out this race since we learned last year at Rochester that running in the rain is not my forte. Chad and Shelly wanted to run against their former teammates, so he had Justine sit out, too.

The rain came back by the starting whistle. The runners disappeared into the mist like you see at the start of a horror movie. You wonder which ones will come back alive.

Justine thanked Coach, declaring, "I hate the way rain messes up my hair."

She approached me with a sheepish look, whispering, "I'm sorry I messed up your thing with Sarah. I didn't mean to. You were so nice to me when I was being a jerk that I thought a kiss would be a good way to say thank you. Forgive me?"

"Sure, I already did that. But Sarah ..."

"I explained it to Sarah, told her about my pranks on the cross country team and how you helped me without telling everybody. She's okay about it now."

What a relief.

When she walked over to get some chocolate, Coach came over.

"Corey, I know you overheard my conversation with Rory in the car. Does that bother you?"

"Kind of, but I know your job is to help other people, too, for the future of the team."

"Yes, that's true, and quite mature of you. See, you are growing into a man. Be patient. Your body will catch up with the rest of you one of these days."

"I wish it would hurry up."

"All in God's time, Corey. Are things going any better in

the rest of your life?"

"Not really. School and home are just crazier than ever. I can't tell you about it now. Too many people around, but pray for me, okay?"

"I will, but you know you could pray for yourself, don't you?"

"That reminds me, Coach, ah, Pastor. Ferdy and I will help with the Trust or Treat, and so will Jimmy and my sister."

"Great!"

Just then a runner zoomed out of the fog—Shelly—lit up with a grin. The two judges, who had spent the whole time talking World Series under the Fogtown tent, hustled over to open the chute. She finished strong, clods of mud shooting out behind her. Turns out she had worn metal cleats, which are allowed in the rain, although no one else had remembered.

We waited a full twenty seconds until two more figures appeared, stiff-arming each other like football players, covered in mud. Though they finished in a tie for second the judge disqualified them both for fighting. A Fogtown Frog took second.

Ferdy came next, and he was right, he did run like a robot, caked with sludge. One by one, they all straggled in, slimy all over. Both teams surrounded Chad, screaming at him, some of them swearing and threatening to beat him up.

"Just try it!" he snarled.

Piecing it all together, Shelly had done her usual jackrabbit thing in her metal spikes, but Chad had started last on purpose. Every time he passed a runner, he would shove them off the track into the drainage ditches. The last Fogtown guy, just as big and mean as Chad, saw what he was doing. When Chad lunged for him, the Frog man wrapped his arms around Chad and they splashed down together, climbed back out, and wrestled to the finish line.

That was the first time I had seen Coach Rusk mad. He

pulled Chad aside, literally, and bellowed at him, "You will go back there, apologize to every member of both teams, then go to your parents' car. And you are suspended from next week's event, you hear. If you pull anything at all like that again, you are off the team."

Shelly was the only clean runner, wet, but clean. Still, she felt dirty. I could see it in her face. I sidled over and said, "You won fair and square, Shelly. You didn't cheat, and you didn't know what he was doing."

"He would have done the same thing to me if he caught up to me."

"No, he would never have caught you. You won fair."

"It doesn't feel fair."

The only person in the whole place who seemed happy was Rory. He sloshed over with his hand in the pocket of his soggy sweatpants.

"Look," he gushed, pulling out a wiggling green thing. "I got a new frog. His name is Calvin."

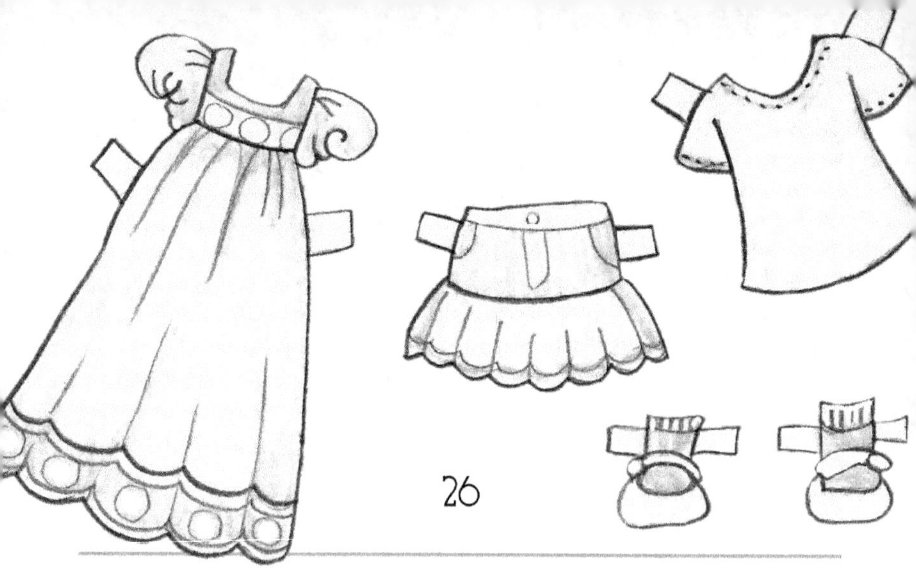

26

PAPER DOLL

A paper doll is what my mother called Kitty and I could see why. When I was four and Sis was almost six, she loved paper dolls. She cut them out very carefully, colored their clothes using all the colors in her 48-stick Crayola box, and tried every combination of outfits. For a while I tried playing with her, claiming that the boy dolls should be dressed by a boy. Trouble was, I was never good at either coloring or cutting. The clothes I cut looked worn out before they were ever worn, and the dolls, well, let's just say they didn't always have all their parts. That made Sis mad. The time I semi-accidentally cut off Ken's head, she hit me. I hit her back. Dad saw it. I got five whacks on my behind—the only time I remember being spanked—before being sent to my room for "a talking to." My sister stuck out her tongue as Dad pulled me past.

He said, "Corey, you will never, ever, hit a girl."

"But she hit me first."

"Doesn't matter. You never hit a girl. Understand?"

I didn't understand, but I never forgot either. That was the last time I ever played with paper dolls or hit a girl.

Kitty was pure white, like she needed Crayolas. Her face, hair, every bit of skin you could see was colorless, even her eyes. She wore a bright red shirt which only made her look whiter.

You'd better be very careful when you touch her, or she might rip.

We were sitting in chairs and on the floor in this tiny trailer. It was clean and neat, but kind of bare. She gave us each a foam cup of instant iced tea with ice cubes. Annie was asleep in the bedroom with the door closed. Kitty was speaking to me.

"Corey, I wanted to meet you. Thank you for sending your pastor to me."

"My pastor?"

"Pastor Rusk. He visited me every day in the hospital. He has been wonderful."

"Coach Rusk?"

"Yes, he said you run really fast. I never could run outside. Anyway, I am so glad to have him and your family as friends now. I never had friends before."

She was almost as small as me and thinner. I blurted out, "How old are you?"

"Twenty-one."

Sis blurted, "And you're a mother?"

"Yes. That is why I asked you all to come. I want to tell you

my story and ask you a big, big favor. Since you decided to take Annie and me into your family, I think you should know more about us."

Her voice was paper thin, too, and I had to listen hard to hear what she said, but she sounded calm and smart.

"Let's begin with the big one. I am an albino. Do you know what that is?"

"You're from Albania?" I answered.

"No, Corey," Mom said. "Albino means you have no skin pigmentation."

I'm glad I didn't ask if she was a Pigmy.

Fortunately, Kitty spoke first. "Yes, no skin pigment, but more. You have to be careful every day. Don't worry, it isn't contagious. It's genetic. But my life has never been normal. One thing is, I have very weak eyes. I've worn glasses since I was Annie's age, thick ones."

I blurted again. "You don't have glasses on now."

I have to stop blurting.

"No, I don't. When I fainted and fell against that chair there, my glasses broke. In the hospital I could hardly see to sign the papers I had to sign. Welfare said they won't buy me another pair because I was careless with them. I should have taken them off before I fell. But that's all right. Pastor Rusk said his church will get some for me."

"You've had a hard life," Dad said.

"You don't know the half of it. The memory I have of my mother is on my fourth birthday. When I asked for a birthday present, she said, 'I'll give you a present all right, you freak. You'll get a new home.'"

"I got all excited, picturing dogs and horses and chickens, like in my coloring book. Instead, she dumped me at the Hanway Children's Home, plunked down my clothes and teddy bear, and told them, 'I'm sick of her. You can have her.'"

At that my mother and sister cried. Dad looked mad. I

looked at my shoes.

"I grew up in foster care, a lot of different houses. I want to thank you for loving Annie, but I don't want her to grow up in foster care. I never felt loved. Some of the homes were nice and the people were good to me. They didn't keep me long, though, because of my special needs. The mean ones kept me longer, because they didn't care about what I needed.

"My big problem is sunlight. Albinos can't be in the sun much, and if we are we need to be covered with clothes, hats and UVA lotion, because we don't tan. We burn. The mean foster parents would say, 'You'll get better if you just get outside and play with the other kids.' They'd push me out the door with no lotion, and latch it shut. I'd try to stay in the shade, but I spent most of my childhood sunburned."

"How could anyone be so cruel?" my mother said.

"I always wondered. I'm told that most foster parents are nice like your family, that I was just unlucky. By the time I was thirteen I developed allergies and asthma, so no homes would take me. I lived for five years at the children's home. When I was seventeen, one of the boys started hanging around me, telling me I was pretty, saying he loved me. I was so glad to hear those words that I let him do anything he wanted."

Sitting in front of Dad on the floor with his hands on my shoulders, I could feel his nails like claws digging into me, but I didn't say anything.

"You poor thing," Mom said.

"It's okay. He disappeared when he turned eighteen, but he gave me my Hermione, the best thing that ever happened to me. I have someone to love and someone to love me. The problem is, it can't last."

"What do you mean?" Dad asked.

"When Annie was born, the doctors ran all kinds of tests. They say I have a severe form of albinism called Hermansky-Pudlak Syndrome."

"That's terrible," Mom said.

"Have you heard of it?"

"No, it just sounds horrible."

"It is," Kitty agreed. She was quiet, calm, no tears, as if she'd used them all up. Sis was using hers up right then. I wanted to, but I'm a boy.

"The doctors say I will probably get skin cancer from all the sun exposure. My blood doesn't clot easy, so I get bruised easy, and if I get a cut I could bleed to death. The worst is the breathing. They say I could live to forty, but probably not."

At that she glanced toward the bedroom.

My father spoke first, more gently than I thought he could. "How can we help you, Katrina?"

She looked at him like a little child looks at her father. I wondered if anybody else ever called her by her real name.

"You're here. Thank you for caring and for loving us. You can do me a really, really big favor."

Dad said, "You have it. What is it?"

"You can adopt Annie, really adopt her, legally."

We were speechless.

"If I'm asking too much, I'll understand, but I don't want her hurt by the system. You should know that she is an albino, too, but much less serious than me. With proper care, she can live a normal life."

Sis got up to hug her first. Mom did, too. Dad and I hugged them while they hugged her. I would have been scared to hug her myself, because I might break her.

"We'll adopt you, too, Katrina, legally, if you will let us," Dad said.

"You would do that? Can you do that?"

"Yes. I've read that adults can adopt adults. Either way, we will always be your family."

"There is one condition to it all."

"What is that?"

"Annie—Hermione—lives with me as long as I can take care of her."

"Done. We'll need to find out how, but we will adopt both of you."

The whole thing was, like, surreal (Sarah's word). Not only was my life changing since I became a teenager, but my whole family was changing. Nobody said anything riding in the Saturn on the way home, except for me.

When we passed the charred remains of another trailer I said, "I think that is where Boo, uh, Vin, uh, Alvin, used to live."

Yeesh, I felt ashamed. If Kitty could survive foster care and Vinny could survive being Booger, what was my problem? I decided maybe I should stop feeling sorry for myself and do something about it.

27

SCHOOL ASSEMBLY

Monday morning, as I was leaving for school, Vinny told me, "I'm gonna be late. They're comin' for me to do more tests, blood tests, DNA, all that crap— sorry. I mean, *stuff*. The docs say that I'm a wonder, livin' like I did, no shots or medicines or good food, but never sick, not even once. Somethin' about anti-bodies and gene-ticks. Should be back to school by lunch."

When I got to school, I found my Buds in the usual spot by the water fountain, waiting for homeroom bell.

"I had a crazy weekend," I said. "How about you?"

"Crazy," said Shelly.

"Boring," Hu grumbled.

"Okay," was the response of Justine and Ferdy.

Sarah had her face down, hands on her forehead. "Way, way too crazy."

"All right, then," I said. "Share the news. Shelly first."

"Chad is mad."

I snorted. "What's news about that?"

"You were there Saturday at Fogtown."

"Four of us were but tell Hu and Sarah what happened."

"Chad got in big trouble. He wore cross trainers instead of spikes, so he got a slow start in the slippery grass. After that, every runner he caught up with he pushed into the ditch."

"You, too?" asked Hu.

"No, I was running jackrabbit in front. But he did it to Ferdy."

Ferdy nodded. "Second time he's done it to me. Won't happen again."

Hu looked a question at Justine and me. Justine said, "Corey and I sat out the race under a tent. Lucky us."

"Anyway," Shelly went on, "when he reached J. D., who used to be his best friend, J. D. dragged Chad into the ditch with him. Chad got suspended from the next meet."

"Oh, yes, that would make him mad," Hu said.

"Yeah. And he's mad at me."

"Why? You didn't do anything."

"Chad thinks he has the right to win every race. I wore my spikes, which the rules allow when it's raining, so I had traction and won the race."

Sarah kind of woke up, and exclaimed, "You won? You won!" She gave Shelly a big hug. "I'm so proud of you."

Just then the loudspeaker squealed. When Principal Farraday used the speaker system he turned it up all the way. He said:

If he wanted to sound like God, this did the trick, except God could have figured out the volume control.

The windows rattled. Students dropped their books to clamp hands over their ears.

Through the open door of Room 137, I glimpsed Mr. Clark diving under his desk. I swear the floor was moving, but the announcements ceased. God does have mercy.

I told my Buds we would continue our stories later. They yelled, "What?"

"Later!"

We fled to homeroom, where we helped Mrs. Sagursky re-shelve her books.

On the way to lunch, Mr. Farraday nabbed me. In a panic, he forgot the dictionary. "That new kid, I mean, that old, I mean, that Alvin Schmidt kid. Where is he?"

"How would I know?"

"You are my spy. I expect you to know."

"Doctor. Tests."

"I need him here, for the Assembly!"

"He said he'll be back."

"He'd better be, or I'll blame you."

At the boys' room door, Noford got me.

"Where's Boo ... Vinny?"

"Doctor. Tests."

"He needs to know somethin' before Assembly."

"He said he'll be back."

"Better be, or else."

"Or else what?"

"Can't tell ya."

When I collected my barbecued Brussels sprouts with zucchini sticks and joined my Buds, they were buzzing like a swarm of bees. In fact, the whole cafeteria hive was buzzing.

"Something is up," I announced.

"Ya think?" said Hu.

Sarah interrogated me. "Principal Farraday grabbed you again. What's up with that? Why you? What do you know that we don't know? Give!"

"I think it's about Booger."

Justine gulped. "Uh-oh, I bet they found his body."

"Something like that."

Just then Chad stomped over, leaving a trail of Brussels sprouts. "I am going to get you geeks. You, too, Shelly. I'll mash you all like this." He dumped his zucchini sticks on the table and pounded them with his fist.

Hu jumped up in front of him. "Why? What did we do?"

Chad elbowed him aside, lowered to me nose to nose, and sputtered, "You got me suspended from cross country. I'm better than you, so you're all tryin' to get ridda me."

Shelly stepped over. "Stop it, Chad. Just stop it."

"You're in it, too, my own sister. You're supposed to be on my side. If I'd caught you, you woulda' been in the mud, too."

"I know that."

"All I got to say is, you better watch your little behinds."

We all watched his big behind travel to the Scuds, where he started grouching with Noford about something or other.

Ferdy inhaled deeply. "Too bad you have to live with that, Shelly."

"He isn't always that bad."

Sarah sighed. "I guess we all have problems we have to live with."

Justine asked her, "What is eating you today?"

"My family, as usual. My mom and dad are fighting. That probably means that my father is fooling around again."

Shelly groaned. "I know what that is like, too."

Sarah clenched both her fists and pulverized the zucchini bits. "Men! You can't trust them!" Then she looked over at Ferdy, Hu and me, and added, "Not counting you guys, of course."

We three future men looked at each other and decided to keep still. I was afraid she had her doubts about us, too. When you consider the Buds, three of us had good fathers, two had bad fathers, and one had only the memory of a father. It makes a difference. Then I realized I had put mine on the good list.

Thank you, God.

ꝏꝏꝏ

At the one-fifty bell, the student body herded down the hall toward the auditorium like sheep to the inevitable slaughter.

Principal Farraday was pacing by the front door. So was Noford.

Suddenly, the social worker's car pulled up, coughed out Vinny, and the principal grabbed him to pull him in the stage door of the auditorium, which he then slammed shut.

Because I stopped to watch, I barely made my assigned seat in the second row before the sound system squawked:

STUDENTS!!!

Fortunately, the vice principal was at the soundboard. She dialed the volume down so we could hear. Our principal must have been flustered still, since he abandoned the r-words for normal talk. Noford and Vinny were perched on the front edge of folding chairs at opposite sides of the podium. The front of Noford's chair bent like rubber while he was leaning forward trying to tell Vinny something in signs and motions.

"Students, I called this assembly because I have important news to impart to you, news you have been anxiously awaiting to hear."

Hanway school is ahead of the times in lunch food, unfortunately, but behind the times in almost everything else, except for video. Our city's only technology store, Electric You, had donated, for the advertising value, an enormous screen and a zoom-lense video camera, which was run by a student volunteer. The picture zoomed in on the principal's red nose and spit-spewing lips. The whole audience turned their heads away.

"Yes, I acknowledge this information is startling. However, you will be encouraged and revitalized. The good news is ..."

We all turned back and leaned forward.

Unlike the video, the sound system is ages old, donated by a defunct radio station. The control board must have a delay switch, because the movement of the gigantic mouth came a little bit before the words, like in a Japanese movie. The three hearing-impaired kids in front of me jumped up before the rest of us.

Principal Farraday's mouth from outer space thundered, *"We have found Booger Schmidt alive!"*

The kids jumped up and down cheering and high-fiving, except for me. I watched as the camera panned to Noford Hammond, who looked like the bad guy in the movies who gets shot and, before he falls, knows that he is dying.

The vice principal had to jack up the sound to a squeal so her boss could be heard.

STUDENTS. ATTENTION.

We all clamped our hands over our ears and stopped yelling.

PLEASE SIT...

The mouth reappeared, like in *Jaws*. We sat, stunned. The volume came back down to just painful.

"First, we have Noford Hammond to thank for his indefatigable efforts to find our lost boy. Noford, please stand."

The camera was too fast for him. He stared at me and drew his finger across his throat. Then he smiled and accepted the applause of the crowd.

When they quieted, Principal Farraday continued, *"I am delighted to announce that, through the exemplary work of our Hanway constabulary and the Federal Bureau of Investigation, Booger has been found in good health and is here with us today. His name is Alvin."*

The whole student body was looking around for a chipmunk. Then the camera panned to Vinny, his eyes wide as balloons, his mouth wide open, the new fillings sparkling in the spotlight like jewels in a crown.

From the back a girl screamed, "That's him, that's him! Vinny is Booger Schmidt!"

28

COULD THINGS GET CRAZIER?

The clamor drowned out even the sound system. Everyone else expressed themselves. Everything from relief and joy to betrayal and rage while I watched Vinny's face. Shock changed to fear, then to brooding, to resignation, and finally, to resolve, with a wicked smile.

The crowd began to chant, like when a baseball star hits a homerun, and the crowd wants them to come out of the dugout for a bow. *BOO ... GER ... BOO ... GER ... BOO ... GER ...*

Principal Farraday had deserted the microphone to hide behind the stage curtain. Vinny rose from his chair, ambled to the lectern and bowed. The room went dead quiet. He leaned into the microphone and said,

"Booger Schmidt is dead ...
Alvin is a chipmunk ...
My name is Vinny.
If anybody calls me Booger ...
... ever again ...
... you will need to explain why ...
... to Noford Hammond."
Noford stood.

The camera moved to him and pulled back to get all of him in the picture. An optical illusion, it must have been, but steam was shooting from his ears.

"Oo-oo-oo-oo-oo-oo-oo." When everyone's air was expelled, nobody breathed.

Vinny said, "Thank you all for caring."

He waved and walked out the stage door.

When everyone inhaled, all the air was used up. We all knew, in an instant, that even if a friend had an enormous, disgusting thing hanging out of his snout, we would need to look for another word to use.

Principal Farraday reappeared at the mike and announced,

"SCHOOL IS DISMISSED."

A cheer reverberated down the halls and by the time it echoed back the auditorium was empty. Nobody wanted to be there if the principal changed his mind.

A few brave souls approached Vinny outside the door, but Noford brushed them away. The Buds reunited at the water fountain and accused me of lying to them.

"You knew it, didn't you, Corey? You knew he was alive, and you didn't tell us."

"I couldn't tell. I was sworn to secrecy."

"How did you find out? Did Farraday tell you on one of your visits to his office?"

"No. I didn't know he knew."

"He's the principal. He knows everything."

"You would be surprised."

"How did you find out?'

Like a suspect under the glaring lights of the interrogation room, badgered by the coppers, I could not stand the heat. I confessed, "He's living in my house."

Their mouths hung open as it sunk in. Sarah shivered. "Oh, Corey. O-o-o-oh."

I tried to explain, but when their mouths hung open, their

ears clamped shut. The girls slunk away. Hu and Ferdy stared at me like I was a possum splattered in the middle of the road. Then Noford, Chad, and Vinny charged down the hall toward me, lining up against us one-to-one.

"You told," yelled Vinny. "You skunk!"

"No. I didn't. Honest."

Noford growled like a rabid dog.

Chad roared, "Don't bother to watch your behinds. I'll blister your behinds from the front." He was hunched down face-to-face with Hu. Hu stepped back and assumed the pose of Ralph Macchio from *The Karate Kid*. I've watched the old movie a hundred times on cable. Chad must have seen it, too, because he backed up a step.

Just then Principal Farraday peeked out the door of his office, looked both ways, and walked over. He ogled Hu and asked, "Young man, are you threatening these fine boys with bodily harm?"

"No, Sir," Hu answered. "I was just showing them one of my moves."

"Good." The principal moved on to Vinny. "I'm sorry, Alvin, to catch you unaware. I wanted to tell you ahead of the Assembly, but you were absent. The FBI revealed your identity to me. I knew, of course, that you would want the entire school to hear the good news."

"Yes, Sir. Thank you, Sir."

The Scuds left, but not before Chad stuck his finger in Hu's face and croaked, "Nice move, kid. I'll show you a few of mine later."

The principal pointed at me. "Zilch. In my office. Now."

Once inside, he was his old self again. "I surmise you suspected this scenario would surface, yet you did not share your surveillance."

"No, Sir. I mean, yes, Sir. I mean I ..."

"Slacking, Zilch, you are slipshod. You should be

severed. Shape up or be sacked."

Whatever that meant, it sounded bad.

"Yes, Sir. I'll try harder, Sir."

"The situation is such that you must assimilate spy standard three: Seize the salubrious solution. Do you have that? Seize the salubrious solution."

I knew "seize" and "solution," but I had to look up "salubrious." My lesson of the month was to "find the best way out." I definitely agreed, but where would I find it?

ꝺꝺꝺ

With all that on my mind at cross country practice, I'm lucky I didn't ram my face into a tree. If I hadn't run with three Bud friends, I might have. They still didn't know what to say, but they steered me through the course.

Afterwards the four of us jogged home together. Justine peeled off to her house first with a, "hang in there, Corey."

Ferdy, before he turned down Sumac Street, said, "Corey, I know you have a lot on your mind, but we only have one more meet before the league championship. Can you still help me win a race?"

"Sorry, Ferdy, I forgot. Let's meet at Butterworth an hour early Saturday. I have an idea we might try."

"I'll be there. Remember, Corey, you aren't just Zilch. You are Zip."

Shelly was the last one. In front of her apartment building, she stopped me to talk. She seemed nervous.

"Corey, you know I like you, don't you?"

"I like you, too, Shelly."

"Is Sarah your girlfriend?"

"No. She just wants to be friends. That's all."

Shelly reached out for my hand.

Yeesh!

She said, "I am so sorry you are having a hard time, and Booger, uh, Vinny's in your house. Corey, you need a friend."

"I have five friends now."

"Maybe you need a girlfriend. I could be your girlfriend."

"Huh?"

"I could be your girlfriend. Do you want to kiss me?"

"Shelly, stop it. I like you. Sarah says that boyfriends and girlfriends break up and can't stay friends anymore. Let's all just stay friends, all right?"

"All right."

She let go.

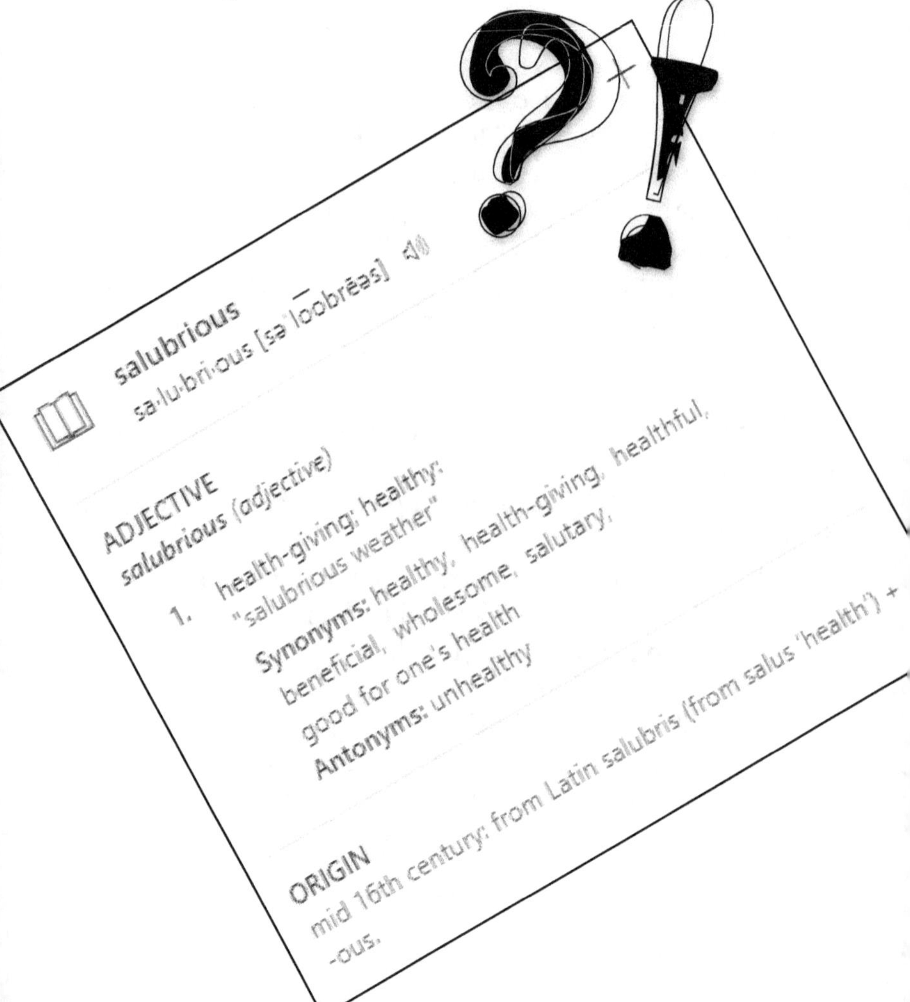

29

TRUST OR TREAT

Trust or Treat was not on Halloween, but on Friday, three days before. Sis and Jimmy were Raggedy Ann and Andy, and Jimmy got the costumes for them. Hu paired up with Shelly as Ninja warriors. Justine and Harley had Roman togas. Sarah and her sister were the non-scariest clowns ever. Ferdy and I didn't have costumes, so we wore our running duds. His sweatsuit was black like a bat and mine was pumpkin orange.

Grace Baptist Church mailed out flyers to all Hanway, advertising:

We workers came at five to set up our areas just inside each classroom door. Some brought pumpkins and other decorations. Ferdy and I brought ourselves, plus treats we bought with money my father gave us. The church provided a big plastic bowl for each room and a box covered with shiny orange gift wrap that had a hole in the top for the kids to reach through and another hole in the back for us to reach through.

When we arrived, we put down our stuff inside the door and looked at the others.

Hu and Shelly took the one-legged pose, the crane, from *Karate Kid.* Hu said, "I taught her that."

"Doesn't scare me," I claimed.

Shelly laughed, "It scared Chad a little. He was mad, and a bit worried."

"You don't really know karate, do you, Hu?"

"Hah! Wouldn't you like to know? The pose is enough to get me out of trouble sometimes. My father taught Kung Fu in China, just so you know."

The Romans and the clowns looked terrific, and so did Raggedy Ann and Andy.

My Raggedy Sister sneered at me. "Why aren't you dressed up?"

"I am."

"I admit you don't need a costume to be a monster, but you could have tried to be a different one than usual."

"Ferdy and I are cross country runners. It's all we had."

Raggedy Jimmy spoke up. "Gee, I wish you said something. My mother has a costume rental business online. We've got a garage full of them. You could have been anything you wanted to be. I'm sure Mom would do it for my friends for free."

"I am something that I want to be, a cross country runner."
"Okay."

We set up. Ferdy and I didn't take long, just filled bowl

with mini-Tootsie Rolls and our box with big ones. By six o'clock when the doors were unlocked for the crowd waiting outside in their cars to stay warm, everybody was ready. The weather was cold with scattered snowflakes. All the little kids had to leave their coats on the kid-level pegs by the door so everybody could see their costumes. A few little angels were weepy about their bent wings.

Still, it was so much fun!

Kids would knock on the door, yelling "TRUST OR TREAT," and we would open up, tell them how cute or scary they were, and offer them "The Big Decision." They could see the mini candy in the clear bowl, but we stopped them from grabbing it until we explained.

"You have a choice. You can take one of these candies you can see, or you can have enough faith to reach in this box and find out if there is anything in there."

If we had more than one kid at a time, we had them all tell us their choices first, then we had those who wanted a mini go first. Then the ones with faith got to reach into the box. Ferdy, with his arm in the hole behind the box, would put a big Tootsie Roll in each kid's hand, so they wouldn't grab a bunch. It also was a little scary to find a hand in there. When the mini-takers would complain, most parents would say, "That's what you chose." If they didn't, I would whisper, "Do the box at the next door."

By the end of the evening our bowl was still quite full. Everybody's bowl was, but the boxes were almost empty.

About six-thirty, the knocker was Annie. I could tell by her Tinker Bell voice. She yelled, "Truck or treat!"

When I opened the door, the voice fit her perfectly. So did the costume. I knew Mom had stayed up late making it. I didn't know what it was, but it had wings.

She looked up, chirped, "Co-ree!" and hugged my leg.

When I told her, "This is my friend, Ferdy," she showed

him the Raggedy Ann doll she brought with her.

"Hi, Furry, this is my bestest friend. Her name is Annie, just like me."

She wanted to snatch a mini from the bowl, but Kitty convinced her to stick her hand in the grab box. When she pulled it out, she asked, "What is it?"

"A Tootsie Roll. It's candy."

She pointed to the bowl. "What is that?"

"A Tootsie Roll."

She pointed to herself. "Big Annie, big Tootsie." The she snatched a mini from the bowl and gave it to her doll. "Little Annie, little Tootsie."

I didn't take it back.

Mom and Dad had brought Kitty and Annie, and they hung around until it was over. Signs advertised door prizes at seven, which kept most everybody there scarfing donuts and guzzling sweet cider. Before the door prize drawing, Coach— I mean, *Pastor*—Rusk, talked with the little kids about the Trust or Treat.

"What was the better prize? Was it what you could see in the bowl, or what you couldn't see in the box?"

The kids yelled, "The box!"

"Did you learn to trust that the secret prize was better than the one you could see?"

"Yes!"

"You learned to have 'faith.' You can't see God either, but, believe me, God is bigger and better than anything you can see. If you trust in God, your life will be bigger and better, too!"

He said a little more, but that's the idea. Then he drew out names for the door prizes—a light-up pumpkin, an enormous teddy bear, a wind-up Batmobile, and a hand-held electronic game called "Pete the Pickle."

While Annie was running around pretending her wings

could make her fly, I smuggled our leftover mini-Tootsies into Kitty's tote bag.

Coach asked Ferdy and I to stay behind to help him clean up. Once we had the tables washed and the floors swept and the furniture back in place for Sunday, we polished off the leftover donuts, four each, and talked.

"Ferdy, Corey, what do you each want the most right now in your life?"

Wow, what a question.

Ferdy said, "Right now I just want to win a cross country race."

Coach said, "You have two more opportunities. You are really close. If only you had a kick at the end."

I chimed in, "I promised to help him with that, starting tomorrow."

"Good. Maybe tomorrow will be the day you will win. Keep me informed how you are doing and ask me if you need help. But Ferdy, have you prayed about it?"

"Well, no. I thought it would be selfish to pray to win."

"Maybe. But you can ask God anything, as long as you trust Him to decide whether to give it to you or not. Why don't you try it right now?"

Ferdy tried it. He said, "God, I know it's selfish, but if it's okay with you, could I win just one race?"

Coach Rusk turned to me. "What do you want, Corey, more than anything, right now."

"I want out of the mess I'm in." Then I laid it all out, brought him up to date. Ferdy knew some of it but was surprised how much he didn't know.

At the end, Coach said, "You know what I think is the worst part for you, Corey? What bothers you the most? You can't stand how it makes you feel about yourself."

I answered, "You're right. I hate having secrets from my friends. I feel like I'm lying without even saying anything."

"I thought so. I have two pieces of advice. First, pray to God for help. Do you want to do that now, like Ferdy did?"

"Yes, I do. Dear God, up in Heaven. I don't know how to pray so I'll just talk to You. I don't like lying, but I'm kind of stuck. Please get me out of this mess. Amen."

"Good. That's what prayer is supposed to be like. My second piece of advice is this: Trust your support structure. Do you know what a support structure is?"

"You mean like in a building, what holds it up?"

"Yes, and you do have a support structure, people who hold you up. You have God and me, but also you have your family and your friends at school. Don't you think the time has come to trust them with the truth?"

"I'm afraid they will hate me."

"They won't. Just trust them."

30

iPOD

My parents could not come to the cross country meet at Butterworth that Saturday. They were meeting a lawyer to get adoption papers drawn up. I understood, but I still felt hurt.

Ferdy and I met at nine. I brought my dad's stopwatch. I found one with the pile of sports gear in the garage. My idea for Ferdy involved his iPod. We sat in winter coats on a park bench, him with his antique earphones, not ear buds, around his neck.

"Ferdy," I asked, "why do you always listen to your music before you race?"

"The music gets me in sync. I choose a song for each race, and listen to it over and over until it's, like, stuck in a loop in my head, so when I put away the iPod before the race, I still have the song. I run the whole race to that beat."

"That's what I thought. So, here's my idea. Think of your five favorites, listen to one of them, then walk over there with it in your head." I pointed to a pine tree about a hundred yards away. "Make a line in the dirt with your toe, and when I give the signal, run back here to the song in your head."

He nodded, left his coat on the bench and did it, five times, once for each song. I timed each one. With him back on the bench, wrapped in his coat, I asked, "Which song was the second one?"

"Let me think." He silently counted his fingers and went back to number two. "That one was *Surrender.*"

"Which one was fourth?"

He went through his fingers again. "*I Want You to Want Me.*"

"Those two were your fastest."

"What was the last one?"

"That was my favorite of all, *The Flame.*"

"That one was the slowest."

"Oh. But I can't give that one up. I feel like the words are my father talking to me."

"Okay. We'll save that one. Today, run your race to *Surrender* and see if you can beat me. But you'll have to do it yourself because I'm not going to let you win."

"I wouldn't be winning anyway if you let me."

About then, the rest of our team arrived, and the Rooster Boosters from Rochester rolled in as a mob. Rochester is in the corner of our state that has more cows than kids. The runners they have, though, are strong and tough. This tribe lives so far from civilization that they don't know how to pronounce the name of their own town. Every other state would say "Rah-ches-ter. They call it "Roo-ster." Plus their team name is the Roosters. Even the girls are called Roosters. So, their fans are called the "Rochester Rooster Boosters." I think they like to come to Hanway so they can go to a MacDonald's. I wonder if they eat chicken sandwiches.

Our whole team was there, but not our whole town. Chad sat, with his back against an elm tree, still mad. Betty Jean's biker dad had his tent set up with kerosene heaters. A frigid wind made me glad I could run to stay warm. When Coach arrived, he had his trunk full of old sweatshirts his church members loaned him for us to wear. Mine said *Minnie's Muffins.*

The big farm boy from last year's meet, the one with the "Bossie" tattoo, wore a t-shirt with no sleeves. If Bossie was cold, she wouldn't tell you.

Ferdy and I ran together in the middle of the pack, working our way forward. He was singing *Surrender* on both the exhale and the inhale, somehow.

"...Surrender, surrender, but don't give yourself away, ay, ay, ay..."

He was running very well. We passed out of the pack to the string of runners out front. By the three-quarter mark, only Bossie was ahead. When we pulled even with the tattoo, he increased his speed to stay with us.

"...Whatever happened to all this season's losers of the year?"

Was it my imagination or did Ferdy speed up as the words did? Yes, he did. Bossie did, too. The time had come for my kick, or they would leave me in the exhaust of their breath. We all burned rubber, like a three-car drag race, and finished in a dead heat. The judge separated us out. Maybe because my legs were moving faster, he chose me number one, Bossie two, and Ferdy three.

Our cluster of Hamster fans burst from the tent chanting, "Zip Zilch, Zip Zilch, Zip Zilch!"

Deja vu. I felt good for my sake, but not so good for Ferdy.

He wasn't bothered. In fact, he was thrilled. "It worked, Zip. I almost did it. I am so close I can taste it."

"Tomorrow," I told him, "we will work on it some more."

Surprisingly, Rory took fifth place and our team squeaked out a win. Shelly had a twisted ankle and limped to her parent's car where Chad sat already.

Ferdy went into the tent for his iPod. He came back out

shouting, "My iPod's gone! Somebody stole it!"

We all looked everywhere without any luck.

Coach Rusk told him, "We can get you another one."

Ferdy said, "You don't understand. That is my father's. They stole my father from me!"

ᎧᎧᎧ

Ferdy was bummed to the max the next day at Butterworth. He said, "I don't know what I'm going to do without my music."

I asked him, "How many times have you listened to those songs over the last six years?"

"Hundreds, maybe thousands."

"Do you know them all by heart?"

"Yeah. Every word of every song."

"When you think of a song, like *The Flame*, do you hear it in your head?"

"I guess I can. Yes."

"Then they stole your iPod, not your music. Your father isn't inside that iPod. He's in your head."

He plunked down on the bench, pulled the fur collar of his coat around his ears and looked into the clouds.

I kept my mouth shut until he came back to looking at me. I said, "Here's what I think you should do. Up to you, of course, but you should play in your head a mixture—faster parts, slower parts, steady beats for your regular pace, parts that change the pace when you feel in a rut—just using each song when you need it."

"Hey, that could work. You are a genius."

"Don't say that until you win a race."

"Only one left to win. Are you okay if I beat you?"

"Only if it's fair and square. I won't give it to you."

"I won't let you."

188

Next morning, Halloween day, I ran to school determined to come clean, to tell the Buds the whole story at the water fountain before homeroom. I never made it.

Principal Farraday got me again.

"Sweets, Zilch, sweets."

"What?"

"The Sellers of the Sweets, who are they?"

Uh-oh. How can I get around this demand without lying.

"Sir," I said, "I seldom see sweet-selling, recently." Two can play his game.

"Surveillance, Zilch. Spy harder. Salubrious solutions. Sink or swim."

"Yes, Sir."

"And Zilch?"

"Yes, Sir?"

"Your surname, Zilch. Is Bobby Zilch your sire?"

"Bobby, Sir? Sire?"

"Your sire—your father—would he be Robert Zilch?"

"Yes, Sir, my father's name is Robert."

He abandoned his "s" words and scratched his right earlobe. His eyes seemed to, like, float back into his brain for a second before zeroing back down on me.

He said, "Bobby Zilch was much better at this spying thing than you are."

PART IV: THE DAMASCUS ROAD

Oh, come on. Read this one.

Saul had his Damascus Road. I had my Halloween Day.

Saul was a flaming bully, a wildfire burning all who got in his way. When you get married and have a kid, don't name him Saul. Name him Paul.

Same guy, different person.

Coach Rusk says God can do that, change a guy's heart completely inside the same body.

Saul was out to get the Christians—grabbing them, beating them up, throwing them in jail—even watching them die. They say that Saul was a little guy, like Napoleon and me. The King Saul in the Bible was a big guy, who kept bullying David, who was the good guy. But Little Saul proved that you don't have to be a big guy to be a bully.

Little Saul ran out of Christians to bully in his own town, Jerusalem, so he jumped on his horse and rode hard toward Damascus, which is, like, 200 miles, to wipe out all the Christians there. Jesus stopped him, shined a million-watt spotlight on him, knocked him flat on the ground, and asked him, "Why are you picking on Me?"

Well, that changed Saul's mind for good. God even changed his name into *Paul,* making him the top superhero on the good guy side.

Coach Rusk says, "God can do that, change bullies into good guys."

I believe it, but I really want to see it.

"I saw the light..."

31

COMING CLEAN

ere's how the humpbacked preacher from Texas had showed it last Sunday: *The stage was dark, except for a spotlight. The preacher, dressed in a Bible-time costume, was raging mad. He was going to get those Christians, every last one of them, get them to give up Jesus or die. Pacing, stomping, yelling, he promised God he would do everything in his power to rid the world of the Jesus Freaks.*

After a few seconds of confusion, I knew this was, like, a play. He called himself Saul, but I knew the preacher's name was really Joe Bob.

The stage was dark again, just a little glow, like moonlight. An orchestra played a country song in the background, "On the Road Again." A faint light came on behind a row of bushes on either side of a boulder. You could hear the clomp, clomp, clomp of hooves, and as the light increased, you could make out a horse with a rider. When he drew even with the rock, the spotlight blazed on him. Saul, who was really Joe Bob, screamed, covered his eyes, and pitched off the horse unto the boulder. The audience gasped, but the sound of his landing was like when you jump into a bean bag. The preacher, propped against the rock, feeling with his hands like he was blind, yelled, "Who are you, Lord?"

A deep voice said, "I am Jesus. Why are you giving Me a hard time?"

Saul said, "Oops, my bad," but I don't think that came from the Bible.

Four more guys in costumes led him away, while a choir sang, "I Saw the Light."

When the preacher came back, he was in a suit. Sometimes in front of the TV, my mind would wander. Not this time. God made Saul into Paul and gave him a brand-new start. That's what I needed to hear.

ǫǫǫ

Back to real life in Hanway School, near blinded by the principal's words about my father, I staggered down the hallway and felt my way into the wrong homeroom. *Oops, my bad.* The bell rang before I found the right one.

My father was Principal Farraday's spy, too? No, that couldn't be!

The whole morning was a blur, like I was hypnotized. My Buds were waiting for me at noon by the lunchroom door. Sarah, yes, it was sweet Sarah, under that halo, her red-hot halo, burned away the scales from my eyes.

"What is wrong with you, Corey? You look like you saw a ghost?"

They led me to our table and sat me down. Dumb means more than stupid; dumb means no words are available when you open your mouth. I was double-down-dumb. I squinted, searched, found four syllables and put them on a word-string: "I've seen the light."

194

"What light? What are you talking about?" Sarah asked.

I took a breath, looked around me, like you do after you have a nightmare, to see whether this world is real.

Friends? Yes.

Cafeteria? Yes.

Real. Yes.

I mumbled, "Could we go to the library? We need to talk?"

Hu looked through the doorway at the menu board. "Let's see. Turnip and tuna casserole with beet bits, or the library? I choose library."

All the Buds agreed.

The librarian, who seems to like having kids in her library, gave us permission to sit around a table in the far corner and talk since we were the only ones there. I began with, "I don't know where to begin."

Justine suggested, "How about with Boo... I mean, Vinny. How in the world did he get into your house?"

I took a deep breath. "You knew that my family started doing foster care. First, we got my baby buddy A-lo. After that, we got my sister's buddy, Annie, because her mother, Kitty, was in the hospital. They are back together now, by the way. My parents decided to adopt them."

"What? They can do that? Both of them?"

"Yes, I'm going to have two more sisters, a little one and a big one. You asked about Vinny, didn't you? My room, I mean the foster kid's room, was empty again, so they said they would send another kid, a boy this time, so I thought I would have a little brother. What did I get? When I knocked on the door of my own room, there he was, cleaned up and named Alvin, but it was Booger Schmidt."

Hu said, "No wonder you started acting even weirder than usual. Why didn't you tell us?"

"I wasn't allowed to tell. Vinny wouldn't let me, and with the police and the FBI..."

"Stop," Shelly said. "You haven't gone back far enough. Why did Booger go missing?"

"His mother's boyfriend beat him up and wants to kill him, so he was hiding in Noford's attic. When the *Where's My Booger* campaign started, and the police investigated, they found him and put him in protective custody."

"You mean Noford knew all along, and he was just lying to the whole school as a way to make money?" Justine said. "The stinker."

"No," Sarah said, "Booger was the stinker. Noford was taking advantage."

I said, "Yeah, he used us, but he was taking care of Booger, bringing him food and all, and if Butch had known where he was, well, both of them might be dead. Noford had a good reason to keep the secret, but he did take advantage."

"You said 'Butch.' Who's Butch?" Sarah asked.

"Butch Roach, the Rest Stop Robber."

"You mean…?"

"Yeah, the other robber, Greta Schmidt, is Booger's mother."

Sarah looks cute when she crinkles up her nose in thought. "That explains a lot. So how did he get to *your* house?"

"Think about it. His mother's in jail and his house burned down. Where's he going to go? The FBI handed him to DCFS, and they handed him to us. He's a foster kid now. At least the cops fumigated him and gave him new clothes."

Hu said, "Yikes, that's like putting a cockroach in a tuxedo."

I groaned. "I've gotten used to it, and I found out he isn't so bad, or so stupid, as we thought. In a way I'm starting to like him a little."

Shelly asked, "Are your parents going to adopt him, too?"

"Yeesh, I hope not. I want my room back. What he really wants is to live with Noford and his Pop."

"Well, that explains a lot more, but not everything," Justine said. "What's up with you and Farraday? Why are you in his office all the time and yet you never get suspended?"

"That's the hardest part. I wanted to tell you, but then again, I didn't. I was afraid you would hate me."

"We might," said Hu. "Try us."

"Okay. Last spring I caught a Twix in the hallway and Farraday caught me."

"Yikes!" Hu said. "You should have gotten three days for that. Why didn't you?"

"He blackmailed me into spying for him."

"Spying?" Sarah asked. "You were spying on us?"

"No! Not on you. On the candy smuggling and anything else suspicious I see. But that isn't the worst of the problem."

"What could be worse than that?" Shelly wondered out loud.

"The Scuds caught me, too. They threatened to tell the whole school about my spying if I didn't keep them informed about what Principal Farraday is doing."

"Yikes squared!" Hu exclaimed. "You're like James Bond gone rogue—Double Agent Corey Zilch."

"Yeah, that's it. I'm a snitch, a spy, a traitor, all that. Do you hate me?"

"No," Sarah said. She even smiled. "I get why you did it. You still should have told us, though. Buds forever, right?"

"But I wasn't loyal and true."

Hu said, "Not true, maybe, but you were loyal in a way, protecting us from the Scuds."

Justine added, "Like you protected me last year from getting humiliated."

Ferdy spoke up at last. "And you've been a lot of help to me."

"If anything," Shelly contributed, "we've gained respect for you now that we know the truth. You should've trusted us.

Sarah asked, "Have you shared this stuff with Pastor Rusk?"

"Yeah. I told him and Ferdy all of this, and even more, on Friday night. Coach Rusk is the one who suggested that I should come clean with you."

Ferdy nodded. "We all have our troubles, don't we? My problem is my stolen iPod. I really need it to have a chance to win the conference cross country meet."

I reminded him, "You have all the music recorded in your head."

"Yep, but I still need my dad's iPod."

Hu stood up and declared, "That's it, then. We are the Buds, and we will stick together to help each other with our problems, and we will stand up to the Scuds together. Agreed?"

"Agreed."

We formed a circle, put our twelve hands together, and shouted, "Buds forever, loyal and true!"

The librarian looked up but didn't shush us. I swear she has ears like a bat, because as we filed out for class, she whispered to me, "I will be praying for you."

32

COMING HOME

My father in his orangey-ness waited for me at the top of the driveway with my neon hoodie in his hand. I threw off my coat and pulled on my pumpkin self.

Vinny had gone with Noford, probably to do some Halloween pranks. I was glad to be alone with my "sire."

Dad was doing better, so we had a good run to the bus bench.

Once we caught our breath, I complained, "Dad, I've been having a rough time in school."

"What's the problem? Classes too hard for you?"

"No, the classes are easy. You saw my report card. No sweat."

"Having trouble making friends?"

"No, I have some great friends, now. We call ourselves the Buds. The problem is that I've been, kinda, sorta, lying to them."

"I thought I taught you not to tell lies."

"Yeah, I know. That's why it bothers me. I haven't really been lying. It's more like I haven't told them the whole truth."

"Same thing. You'd better lay it all out for me. When did

this start?"

"Do you remember when I fell in the creek near the end of sixth grade? I didn't really fall. I was thrown in by two bullies. That's why I took up running, so I could get away from them."

"Fight or flight, huh? Flight is a good choice for you at your size."

"After that I helped Sarah escape from them, so we became friends, and she added her friend Hu. You've met him. And we kept adding friends until we are six Buds now."

"Safety in numbers, yes. Good strategy."

"Trouble is, the bully bunch has grown, too, into six. We call them the Scuds, after those missiles from the Iraq War. The Scuds are, like, the enemies of the Buds."

"An even match, six against six."

"Not really so even. They are bigger and tougher than we are. Good thing we're smarter."

"Mistake number one. Never underestimate your enemy. They may well be smarter than you think. Still, what you are describing is normal stuff for middle school."

"Not anymore. It got complicated. The Scuds have started a kind of business. Stealing lunch money wasn't enough for them, so they took up candy smuggling. Do you remember the First Lady's healthy-kids campaign, when Mom and Sis were with her on TV last year?"

"How could I forget? I never laughed so hard ..."

"Well, it's still going. You know what they served today? Turnip tuna casserole with beet bits."

"Ugh."

"Candy is banned by the school board. They'll suspend you if you are caught with a candy bar. Do you know what the most valuable treasure is at school now?"

"Candy, of course. In my day it was cigarettes."

"The Scuds make big money selling candy, plus they've

got other things, like the *Where's My Booger* campaign. They made a fortune on those t-shirts and the Booger Bands."

"Oh, yes, how did that turn out? Did they ever find that Booger kid?"

"They did. I'll get back to that in a minute. Do you remember Principal Farraday?"

"Oh, boy, do I."

"He remembers you, too. He asked me if I was Bobby Zilch's boy."

"Everybody called me Bobby back then."

"Mr. Farraday is determined to catch the 'mischievous miscreants' who are breaking school law with their 'miserable merchandise'..."

"Still talks that way, huh?"

"He's on the 's' words now. Anyway, I was walking down the hallway on the way to lunch one day when a Twix bar flew at me. I caught it without thinking and Principal Farraday saw. He dragged me into his office and threatened to suspend me if I didn't start spying on the other kids."

Dad's head whipped up and his chin dropped down. "You're kidding."

"I'm not. Then the Scuds grabbed me and threatened to expose me as a snitch if I don't spy for them, too."

"You're kidding."

"So, I've been snitching on them, each to the other, telling them as little as I can get by with rather than all that I know, trying to keep it a secret from everyone else, and it feels like lying, and I just want to find a way out of the whole mess."

"You're kidding."

"No, I'm not. Then this morning Mr. Farraday said something really weird. He said, 'Your father was much better at spying than you are.' Dad, what did he mean by that?"

"Corey, my son, I have two things to say to you right now. First: Atta boy! You are a chip off the old block! And second, let's go tell your mother!"

He jumped up, pulled me with him, and we ran home.

Bursting through the door, Dad yelled, "Marie! Marie! Where are you? Come here!"

Mom exploded out of the kitchen, hands coated in flour, holding a chicken wing. Sis scrambled along behind her with a half-peeled apple.

Mom screamed, "What's wrong? Who's hurt? Grab the phone, Sis!"

Dad said, "No, no, nothing's wrong. I've got good news."

Mom let out a sigh and said, "Well, spit it out. We've got water boiling."

Dad spit it out. "Our son is The Mole!"

"My little boy is The Mole? That can't be."

"No way," said Sis.

I had no idea what they were talking about.

Dad turned me toward him, put a paw on each shoulder, panted a little, and barked out his words. I hoped he wasn't planning to lick my face.

"You are The Mole, Corey. You have struck gold. Why are you keeping this a secret?"

"I don't want everybody to hate me."

"Hate you? Hate you? You don't know what The Mole is, do you."

He was right about that. I said, "A mole is like a rat that lives underground. I don't want to be a rat, and I hate being underground, so I don't want anybody to know what I am doing."

"Hah. I thought so. You've got it all wrong. The Mole is an opportunity, a coveted honor at Hanway School. I was The Mole twenty-five years ago."

Sis said, "Jimmy was The Mole last year."

Mom's eyes glazed over. "I fell in love with your father when he was The Mole."

Sis added, "The girl's love The Mole. They all wanted Jimmy. I got him."

I collapsed unto the sofa. "I ... don't ... get ... it ... at ... all."

Dad explained, "The Mole is legendary at Hanway. Every year Farraday picks one boy to be his spy. He thinks the students don't know. But when they figure out who The Mole is, you have the opportunity to be a superhero."

"How?"

"If you're good at it, you become a buffer between the student body and Principal Farraday, who is, well, you know it by now, rather dense and unbending. You keep them out of trouble by giving them advanced warnings, and you 'leak' things to Farraday that the students want him to know, as if they don't want him to know, of course, so that keeps the complaints anonymous so that nobody gets blamed. All the time the big guy thinks he is putting one over on those 'inferior ingrates.' It's a game, son, and you need to learn how to play it."

Mom edged over and leaned her cheek on Dad's shoulder. "Your father was a wonderful mole. He became the most popular boy in school, and I was the girl who got him. Permanently."

"How come nobody ever told me about this?"

Sis answered, "Nobody ever thought you could be The Mole."

"What if I don't want to be popular?"

"Tough luck," Dad said. "The Mole is a calling. You have no choice. The other kids need you, so you do what you have to do. Think of it as a chance to do a lot of good for your fellow Hamsters. Don't you want to do good for people?"

"Yeah, I want to be good at what I do. So far, I haven't

done much. Mostly, I want to feel good about myself. I want to be an honest person, to tell the truth."

"Good. You will be telling the truth to the students, and telling the truth to the principal, and that will make the whole school better. We can help you with that."

"Okay. I'll be The Mole. But what should I do about the bullies, the Scuds?"

"No one can blackmail you once the truth is out."

"There is something else you guys should know. Do you remember the big deal about *Where's My Booger*? Booger was one of the two guys that threw me into Weasel Creek."

Mom said, "The poor, pathetic thing. They say he stunk so bad even the teachers wouldn't go near him. I suppose he is at rest now, dead and buried in some woods somewhere, but his soul is in heaven. Maybe God gave him a bath on the way in."

"More like a shower," I said.

"No, he isn't dead," Dad told her. "Yesterday's paper had a small article on the last page about him. They found him safe and sound, and he's back in school now, under a different name, I forget what."

"Vinny," I told them. "His new name is Vinny, and he is at rest all right. He has been at rest in that room, right there, for a week now. His real name is Alvin Schmidt."

"Alvin is Booger Schmidt!" Sis dropped her apple and ran for the bathroom. She slammed the door. I had never before heard such noises from her.

000

Her first bout of nausea behind her, Sis called Jimmy, offering him honey ham, cheesy potatoes and apple pie if would come over for supper. In between bites I told my story a third time.

"Cheez wiz," he said. "You have made a mess of things. You need to do what I did, embrace The Mole."

I shivered at the thought.

Dad agreed. "That's what worked for me."

Jimmy said, "Instead of trying to hide what you are, you should make it obvious. But you can't just stand up and announce that you are The Mole. They wouldn't believe you."

"I still can't believe it," Sis said.

Dad said, "What you need to do is ham it up. Overact it, so they can't ignore it."

Jimmy took over. "Once the other kids know you are The Mole, they'll get behind you. That will make everything easier."

"Jimmy," I objected, "I'm not like you. You're good at talking. You think quick. You're good at everything."

"Except math," Sis said.

"We'll pass math together, you little thinker," he said back to her.

I said, "You're a natural, Jimmy. I'm not. I stutter over what to say and then think of it when it's too late to say it. I don't have your kind of presence. I have an absence."

"That was pretty good." Jimmy replied." You shouldn't put yourself down, Zip. Besides, you don't need to be a good talker to be The Mole, but you need to be a good listener. That's what everybody wants, somebody to listen, somebody who cares what they think."

"You should run for President some day," I said.

"Then I could run for First Lady," Sis said.

"Whoa," Dad said, swallowing hard. "I wasn't a good talker, either, but I was a darned good actor. You could do what I did, set up a drama and overact it. That will convince them."

Mom beamed. "When he walked into the lunchroom as Superman, I tingled all over. When he was Clark Kent, I wanted to be Lois Lane. We ended up being Robert and Marie

Zilch, but I still think we're happy ever after."

"Gag me with a spoon," said Sis.

I thought, *Superman's not dope nowadays, plus I don't have the right build.*

I said, "I don't know how to act, but Sarah does. Maybe she could coach me."

"Sure," said Jimmy, "you could even get your friends to help pull it off in, like, supporting roles. Dude, you'll be a star!"

"Maybe a shooting star," Sis muttered.

"We can all help out," Jimmy said. "I'll get my mother to help out with costumes. She gets bored when business is slow, and she'll have fun with this, though she might want to get a job as a lunch lady so she can watch."

Sis said, "Well, I suppose if I have to, I could write it out like a play, you know. I get A's at that in communications class."

So, my whole family helped me plan the strategy to dig me out of the mole tunnel I had dug for myself. My sister, as sarcastic as ever, did seem to enjoy herself. I don't think she had ever seen me as a person before, just a pest.

I decided to share the plan with my Buds the next day, take another day for rehearsal, and the opening act would be Thursday.

Then my sister sent up a flare. "Are you going to tell that Booger creature in there?"

"His name is Alvin," Mom corrected.

"He wants to be called Vinny," I said, "and no way! I don't want the Scuds to know, and Vinny is one of the Scuds!"

33

THE PLAN

Vinny came home by nine-thirty, his curfew. He seemed to like having rules and a family that cared about when he came home. He slid the bolt at the top of the stairs and came down. He stuck his face through the open doorway and grunted. "I vant to drink your blood."

I was in my pj's doing homework. He was Dracula, with fangs and fake blood dripping down his chin. I reached for the silver cross hanging above my bed and hugged it to my heart.

"You should'a gone with us, Corey. We scared the, uh, *heck* out of a bunch of little kids. Noford was Wolf Man. You could'a been… oh, never mind. You wouldn't scare nobody no matter what you put on."

"Mighty Mouse. I could be Mighty Mouse. Here I come to save the day…"

"Mighty Mouse? Never heard of him."

"Old cartoons. All that my mom would let me watch when

I was little was old cartoons.”

“You don’t even know how to have fun, do ya? Your mother never let ya.”

“So did you come down here to make fun of me?”

His face went serious, fangs and all. “No, I came down here to warn ya. Chad is out to get ya, and Chad is, like, Jason without the mask.”

“Who is Jason?”

“Da—I mean, *dang,* you don’t know much. You grow up in a box? You don’t wanna mess with Jason, and you don’t wanna mess with Chad. He ain’t just after you. He’s after your buddies, Hu and Ferdy, too.”

“Why are you telling me? Aren’t you and Chad on the same side?”

“Not really. You and your family have treated me decent. I wish I could start up again and not be so nasty.”

“That’s okay, Vinny. My dad would call it ‘water under the bridge.’ Why do you stick with that gang, anyway, now that you’re Vinny?”

“S’where I belong. I ain’t goody-goody. I wouldn’t fit with your friends, for sure. Things are better now that I’m Vinny. Kids that used to look down on me look up at me. They’re scared of me. I like it.”

“You like people being afraid of you?”

“Yep. I do. ‘Cept for Noford and Pop, all I ever got was hate. Greta hated me, and the scuzballs she brought home beat on me and did nasty other stuff to me. I was always the scared one until now.”

“Seeing the police and FBI hauling you out of school didn’t hurt either. What’s up with that anyway?”

“Told ya, I’m a witness. Butch and Greta crossed state lines. That brought the Feds in. So, when I told ‘em about the men what messed with me, and who they is, they got very interested.”

"Wow. You are kind of important now, aren't you."

"Guess so. And gettin' even is so sweet. The cops don't think I'll have to testify since they got them all dead to rights. Greta turned state's witness already, took a plea for ten years in prison on condition she spill all the…uh…beans."

"So, you don't have a mother anymore."

"Never did. No father, neither. Makes me a bit jealous at you, ya know, with your perfect family, like. But that's changin' some, too. Gonna have a father. Noford's Pop wants me."

"He does? But he gets in trouble, too."

"Only when he drinks. Bar fights. He's good to Noford and me. 'Sides, I got a secret I can't tell ya yet. Anyhow, I think I'll be movin' out soon."

ᴏᴏᴏ

Hard to believe all this stuff happened on one Halloween Day. The next day I shared the plan with the Buds. They were like kindergarteners who got a box full of puppies. They each wanted a role to play.

Other than that, November 1 was an ordinary day, but for the fact that the school was freezing. Mr. Sledgehammerhead could be heard banging pipes in the furnace room.

The Vice Principal made up letters for us to take home, saying that we should all bring jackets and sweaters until they got it fixed.

Wednesday was colder yet. Lunch was asparagus yogurt over whole wheat pancakes, which actually was edible, and everybody ate them while they were hot, for the warmth.

To top it off, before the afternoon bell, the Vice Principal, who knew how to work the volume control, announced:

210

"Students. School will be held tomorrow. Heating experts have been summoned and will be working this afternoon. Please wear warm clothes in layers until further notice. As for today, school is dismissed."

The cheer was deafening, though shivery. Some went to their lockers for cell phones to call for rides. The rest waited outside for an emergency run of the buses, where the sun was out and it felt warmer. Sarah and I snuck into the auditorium for my first acting lesson.

"Corey," she said, "an actor acts with the whole body, not just the voice. Your face, your hands, the way you stand, and the way you move are just as important as what you say."

"That's good," I answered, "because I don't want to say very much."

"Good thinking. Keep it short and simple."

She put me on the stage while she stood in the aisle. The plan was for me to be a different character each day during lunch hour. We had chosen the first five, and we would see where it would lead from there. Sarah walked me through each one—how he would stand, how he would move, what expression would be on his face, what he would say, if anything at all—until I got it right. I had two hours of drama practice before it was time for cross country practice.

At the end she climbed up on stage to give me a good long hug. With her arms still around me, she said, "I'm just trying to get warm."

"Me, too," I murmured through her waterfall of hair in my face that smelled like lilacs.

"You passed the test," she whispered.

"The acting test?"

"No, the kissing test."

"What?"

"You've been honest with me, so I need to be honest with you. You aren't going to like it. So could you maybe forgive me even before I tell you?"

"I guess."

"I put Shelly up to it."

"What?"

"I convinced Shelly to try to get you to kiss her."

"Why?"

"I'm sorry. I just had to know that I could trust you."

"So, I passed?"

"You did. But Corey, don't expect to kiss me for a long, long time, okay? I want us to stay friends."

I agreed, but...

How long will it be?

34

FACEDOWN

Thursday, at lunch, I was Sherlock Holmes, the old version, in the long coat, cape, deerstalker hat, and pipe. I only hoped I wouldn't be suspended for bringing an empty pipe into school. Sarah was Dr. Watson, the modern version, except that for fun she stuck a moustache under her nose. She made notes in a notebook, like she was recording clues for when she would write up the story. She would show them to me every so often, but really it was my clue about the next thing to do or say.

I stalked around, looking through my giant magnifying glass at the avocado custard tarts, whispering in her ear, and she would write the next clue. Gradually the talk and the laughter got louder and louder, until with the room in an uproar we walked back out the door. When we came back without our costumes, we got a standing ovation.

On Friday, I was Batman, with the full costume, and Shelly was Cat Woman. Boy, was she slinky! She got whistles. I got thumbs up. We just stood against the wall, poker-faced, hands on our hips. The Scuds stared. Chad was getting madder and madder. Suddenly he stomped up to within an inch of his

213

sister's face.

"You think you're hot stuff, huh? Well, I don't, and I say it's time for this to stop."

Shelly shimmied sideways along the wall and Hu came out of nowhere to get between the two of them.

"You leave her alone!" Hu yelled. "She's a girl. Back off!"

"Yeah, I noticed. Who's gonna make me back off?"

"I am."

"Sure, you are."

He motioned to the rest of the Scuds to come over. Noford groaned, but he got up, so the others did, too. Then Ferdy, Justine and Sarah joined us, lined up face to face with the Scuds, six on six, away from the wall. The Studs, mostly football players, moved to the back table to give us space, then backed up to watch. All the other kids crowded in front of them so they could see.

Hu was in front of Chad, ripping off his winter coat, throwing it behind him on the floor. He said, "I can move easier without this."

Chad said, "Don't matter. You're not gonna get away before I squash you." He took off his leather jacket and threw it over Hu's.

Shelly and I just had our costumes, which were not going to come off, but all the other Buds and Scuds tossed their coats on the pile, too. One of the Bosley's stepped in front of Shelly and the other in front of me. I stared him… her… *it*…in the eyes. I had never heard either Bosley say a word. I didn't even know that they could talk. Plus, their faces were always blank, until now. The one I was staring at smiled, puckered up and made a kissing sound. I did not find it attractive. I didn't even know whether this one was the boy or the girl. Either way was creepy.

I said, "I can't hit a girl."

Justine said, "I can," and switched places with me. which left me face to face with Vinny.

Sarah was face to face with Amy. Ferdy got Noford.

Noford said, "Chad, you don't want to do this."

Chad answered, "I think I do."

Amy whined, "Nofie, I don't want to fight."

He said, "Don't worry, Babe. I'll protect you."

I whispered to Vinny, "Do you want to do this?" He shook his head.

That's when Noford took charge. He commanded, "Chad, don't do it. Three of us are playing in the big football game tomorrow. We get in trouble, we can't play. You are on your own with this one." And he and Amy turned and went back to the table. The Bosley's and Vinny followed them.

"Don't matter," said Chad. "I can do this myself."

Hu took up his *Karate Kid* position.

"What are you," Chad sneered, "a pigeon?"

"A vulture," Hu answered.

"More like a flutterby. I'm gonna rip off your wings and feed them to you. Then I'll use you like a rag to wipe up these other dweebs."

Hu said quietly, "Listen to Noford, Chad. You don't want to do this."

"I sure do," he yelled. He made a fist, wound up, lunged forward and swung.

So fast I could hardly see it, Hu grabbed the fist, dipped down, shifted his weight and made an animal sound. Chad flew up and over. Under his legs I spotted Principal Farraday entering the cafeteria. *Wham!* Chad landed face-down on top of the pile of coats. The room shook and the table rattled. *Whooooosh,* the air left Chad's lungs. He lay still with his eyes and lips moving silently.

Principal Farraday demanded, "What's going on here?"

Hu smiled and answered, "Just showing Chad another one

of my moves."

"Is that right, Chad?"

He gulped in air and nodded.

ꚙ

The state Middle School Football Championship game was played the next day at Hanway High school.

The game is big, just not as big as it sounds, since our state has only two leagues that play football in middle school. Most don't play football until high school. Some do-gooders are trying to outlaw middle school football, but our state government can't agree enough to pass any laws, unless it involves raising taxes.

Coach called off cross country practice, if we would promise to sit together at the game. We were early enough to get prime seats in the front row right near the Hanway team bench.

Ferdy was sitting with Justine. Hu came to the game to sit with Shelly. My sister surprised me by coming with Jimmy, who was the star of the team last year and never missed a game. I sat next to him. Sarah didn't come. After me, down the row, were Tyler, Betty Jean, and the others. Chad was missing, and so was someone else, but I couldn't remember who.

Chad came in late, shuffling like an old man, and eased down at the end by Coach Rusk.

I heard Coach ask, "What's wrong with you?"

Chad answered, "I took a bad fall."

Coach said, "You should be more careful."

Our team was playing the Fitzroy Wildcats, from the southern edge of the state, where they do have wildcats in the State Forest. Fitzroy brought one in a cage with a sign over it saying "Fritz." We had won our league, and they had won theirs, so this was for top dog, or cat, or hamster. Fitzroy was

216

big and mean. Noford was our biggest and meanest.

I heard Chad tell Coach Rusk, "I've had it with cross country. I quit. Next year I'll play football." He got up and moved to a spot behind the cheerleaders.

Hammy, our Hamster Mascot, was bouncing all over the field bothering everybody. Ferdy played Hammy last year, in a bigger costume which had met an unfortunate accident with me inside it. This one was smaller, better fitting, more cartoonish, and this Hammy was more of a ham. He danced over to the caged Fritz, stuck his purple tongue out and gave it a raspberry. The wildcat screeched and bit the tongue off. Good thing it was fake.

The kickoff solved the mystery of why Tori Bosley was on the team. She was the kicker. They let the girls do that, and boy, I mean wow, was she good. She kicked the ball into the end zone for a touchback, and the game was on.

Tommy Bosley was good, too. Fast, quick-footed, running behind Noford at right guard, he gained at least five yards every run. When he sprinted to the outside as a receiver, he caught every ball thrown to him. In school the Bosleys were like walking posts. Playing football, they came alive. Tommy scored, Tori kicked, 7-0. Tommy scored, Tori kicked, 14-0. At least, I assumed it was Tori doing the kicking. That could have been Tommy, too.

Tori and Tommy wore the same number, thirteen. I mentioned it to Jimmy.

He said, "Yeah, my friends tell me that they wouldn't play unless they both got the same number, and it had to be thirteen."

"Is that allowed?"

"Yeah, as long as they are not on the field at the same time, and the Bosleys never are. You can see why Coach Haggerty gave in."

"Weird."

"Right. But that's the Bosleys. They do everything together."

Unfortunately, the Bosleys and Noford didn't play defense, so the Wildcats scored easily, too, and by halftime the score was 21-21.

During the intermission, the band played, and the cheerleaders cheered without knocking over the watercooler. My sister was in high school now, which took all the fun out of it. Hammy retrieved his mangled tongue that the wildcat had spit out of the cage, disappeared, and returned later with it stapled to his bottom lip.

As the teams ran onto the field for the second half, Hammy, who was constantly chattering in a muffled way, danced over to Fritz, used both paws to stick out the limp purple tongue, then turned to give Fritz the moon. Fritz promptly bit the tail off.

On the kick-off, after the whistle signaled the play dead, a Fitzroy player flattened Tori. The ref called a foul, but that didn't help Tori, writhing on the ground. I guess Fitzroy's strategy was to knock the kicker out of the game so they could win on extra points. Tommy ran out with Coach Hardesty to help her off the field and in the school door. Coach Hardesty came back alone.

With the Bosleys gone, Fitzroy ran up the score to 35-21. Our substitute kickers and runners were not very good, and the receivers kept looking up at the huge Wildcat tacklers and kept dropping the ball. Near the end of the third quarter, two number thirteens walked out of the school arm-in-arm, to the cheers of the Hanway crowd. One of them was limping. One left the other on the bench and went to receive the kick from Fitzroy.

He was mad. He caught the ball, juked left, ran right, and stiff-armed any Wildcat that came close, littering the field with them before gliding over the goal line. He ran back to the bench, danced in circles around Tori, and the two of them, plus Noford, huddled with the coach. Finally, Tori limped out to kick the extra point.

The limp had disappeared by the time she blasted the kick-off in a line drive right into the returner's chest, knocking him down. She was obviously mad, too. When he got up with the ball and tried running down the sideline, it was Tori who leveled him like a bulldozer rolling over a ragweed. Coach Hardesty sent Noford in on defense for the first time. Three plays in a row Noford plowed through the line to nail the quarterback. Fitzroy had to punt.

Coach used short passes and runs to push the ball down field through most of the fourth quarter, using Tommy sparingly, maybe to save his strength. Finally, we scored on a quarterback sneak behind Noford, Tori kicked, and the game was tied thirty-five all.

Fitzroy got the ball back and was moving it when Hardesty sent Noford back in on defense. He plowed through the line, batted the ball out of the running back's clutches and fell on it. That football would never be used again. They had to get another one. Now we had a minute left to score from sixty yards away.

I looked down the bleachers at my row. Jimmy was holding my sister's hand, Ferdy was holding Justine's, and Hu was holding Shelly's. Boy, I missed Sarah.

Our tight end caught a pass for ten yards. On a busted play, our quarterback gained five before running out of bounds to stop the clock. Tommy's turn. At the snap he cut right, then left, ran right toward Jimmy and I, then pivoted for the pass, which was already on the way. He jumped high, snatched it out of the air, and landed just as the defender arrived. The Wildcat clawed at his shirt, pulled the shirttail out, and yanked it up his back for a split second. Tommy pulled loose, yanked the shirt down, and ran backward five yards until falling out of bounds.

I asked Jimmy, "Did you see that?"

"Of course, I saw that."

"Do you think Coach Hardesty knows?"

"Of course, he knows."

"Why would he go along with it?"

"The high school coach is retiring. Hardesty wants the job."

To win it we needed a forty-yard field goal. I watched number thirteen get up slowly and limp unto the field. I kept my eyes glued on that same Bosley the whole time, until the same thirteen kicked the ball between the goal posts, and Hanway won the game.

Hammy ran over flapping his loose purple tongue. "Did you see that, huh, how Tommy caught that ball. I'm gonna do that when I'm in eighth grade. I'll run like the wind, fly like a bird. I can do it, don't you think, don't you think. I can run that fast. I can jump that high. I know I can, I know I can."

Now I knew who it was I had missed from the cross country team.

I watched the Bosleys arm in arm again. One of them was limping. At last, I put it all together. Tommy was Tori, and Tori was Tommy, both could kick, and the star running back of Hanway's champion football team was a girl.

I asked Jimmy, "Are you going to tell?"

"Not me. Are you?"

"I'm not a snitch."

35

FATHERS

Our family was all together for Sunday dinner, including Kitty, Annie, and Vinny Schmidt. Mom made a huge pot of spaghetti, or as Annie called it, "bug-sketti," plus carrot cake. If Hanway School would just hire my mom to plan the menus and cook, kids wouldn't want to fight in the cafeteria instead of eat.

We were celebrating our new family members. Annie had done wonders for my sister, the picky eater. Annie put the end of a bug-sketti worm in her mouth, said, "I'm a itty-bitty robin birdy," and slurped it in. The noodle wiggled, flinging sauce on her face and everywhere else.

Kitty yelped. "Annie, you're making a mess." She turned to Mom and apologized. "I'll clean it up," she said.

Mom answered, "Nonsense. We are a family. We will all clean it up."

Sis surprised me with "I'm a bigger birdie." *Slurp.* She and Annie giggled nose to nose.

Dad flapped his wings and said, "I am Big Bird." *Slurp.*

Soon we were all doing it, including Vinny. By the end of dinner, we all had a bad case of the washable measles.

Kitty said, "I never laughed like that before in my whole life.

Vinny said, "So families are like this, huh?"

My crazy family is crazy good, isn't it?

Finally, Dad put on his serious face. "Official business." He turned to Kitty and Annie. "Do you Katrina and Hermione, take this Zilch family as your beloved clan, to have and to love from this day forward?"

"We do," Kitty answered in a solemn tone. Annie giggled.

"Do you, Zilch family, promise to love, honor and eat bug-sketti with Katrina and Hermione until death do us part."

"Yes!" we all shouted, except for Vinny, who seemed choked up.

"It's official then, except for the paperwork and judge. I now pronounce you Zilchkins."

"Yay!" We all hugged and shared measles, except for Vinny, who seemed to need to cough.

Kitty asked, "What should I call you? I've never had a real father."

"Call me Dad, Papa, Daddy, Pop, Robert or Hey You, whatever you want to call me. Just call me when you need me."

She turned to my mom and asked her, "Since Annie calls me Mommy, so I don't want to confuse her, what should we call you?"

Mom thought a minute. "Why don't you just call me Mother, and Annie can call us Mama Marie and Papa Bob.

Kitty coached Annie a bit before she could say "Papa Bob," but Mom's name in Annie's mouth always came out "Mama Me-me."

"That'll do," Mom declared, as she dished up and passed out plastic goblets of chocolate mousse.

Dad continued our family meeting with a report that the lawyer expected the process to be brief since we had no custody problems, Katrina was a responsible adult, and the judge was bound to be sympathetic. The lawyer confirmed that Kitty could keep her medical card and welfare income, and since Annie was in the DCFS system now, some benefits would follow her as an adopted child.

I kind of zoned out, wondering how I would feel right now if I was Vinny, not being adopted. Kitty was the one who turned to him to say, "Are they going to adopt you, too?"

Sis choked on her mousse.

As Vinny opened his mouth, Mom jumped in. I mean, she spoke first. "We don't need to adopt Alvin. He has some good news of his own to share."

Vinny wiped his face with his napkin and cleared his throat, like it had something stuck in it. "I have a father already. I never knew it for sure, but I wondered. The DNA test came back positive. Noford's Pop's my Pop. Noford and me's brothers, half-brothers.

"Pop spelled it out yesterday. He got two girls preggy in high school, but he could only marry one. He married Noford's mom, but she ran off with another guy after he was born. Pop told Greta he'd never get hitched again, so she started drinkin'. That's why Pop kept bringin' us food and stuff and took me in his place when things was bad.

"When DCFS caught me, he told 'em the whole story, and they took tests to, like, prove he wasn't lying just to get me as a kinda slave in his garage. Pop and Noford don't get sick neither, just like me, so that was a clue. It's gena tick. Now the DNA says it's so. Don't need no lawyer or judge or nothin'. That's why I'm here right now. Pop and Noford's fixin' up a room today to surprise me, like as if I don't know. I don't gotta sleep on no floor like I use ta. Gonna have a bed of my own in a real house."

Before we ran in Butterworth, I told Ferdy all about what happened in my house at Sunday dinner, including Vinny's news. His response was, "I had a good father for a while at least. Still do, really. I just wish I could see him."

"Do you ever feel like he is with you?"

"Sometimes. I dream about him a lot. I hate it when I wake up."

"Ferdy, I've been thinking about your music and your running. You always run to the beat of a song. Why just one?"

"I don't know. I guess because that's what my father did."

"But he wasn't running a race, was he?"

"No. He just ran to keep in shape."

"You had a favorite song that was slower than the rest."

"Yeah. *The Flame.*"

"Would you sing it for me?"

"If I had my iPod, I could bring it up for you to hear."

"Ferdy, I know you have it memorized. Just sing it."

He did, and he had a really good voice. Maybe he could grow long hair and join Cheap Trick. I listened carefully. The part that got to me was about feeling lonely and *I can't believe you're gone* and a response, like his father was singing it back to him. *Wherever you go, I'll be with you… I will be the flame.*" Ferdy really got into it. When he was finished and caught his breath, he explained.

"Before my father left for the war, he snuck me into a Cheap Trick concert outdoors. I was only seven. He was tall and he lifted me onto his shoulders for the whole concert so I could see. The last song was *The Flame.* He had brought two lighters and he handed one to me and used one himself. We held them high, side by side, and sang *I will be the flame.*"

I said, "That's our answer. Do you know what double-time means?" He did.

You take shorter steps, but two for every one beat. The cross country meet would declare a team champion, but it really was a race of individuals. You couldn't follow a team strategy when you were competing against five other teams, so we laid out a strategy for Ferdy to run his own race. The course at Sumac is also longer than our Butterworth trail. We remembered the landmarks from last year's race, so we chose a different song for each leg of the course, ending in *The Flame*, in double time.

This wasn't the way I would do it for myself, but this race wasn't about me. We ran it as we imagined it in the high school course. It worked. I could barely keep up with him at the end.

As we parted I told him, "You practice that every day this week and you might just beat me on Saturday. But no gimme's, you understand?"

"No gimme's."

ꝺꝺꝺ

That night, Vinny came down to see me. He said, "I'm 'bout packed up. You can have your room back tomorrow."

I said, and I meant it, "I'm glad you have your own family now."

"I'm sorry that I was so mean to you, throwin' you in the creek and all. I didn't want to, but Noford's got this power thing, ya know, and he's my only friend, ya know, so I go along with him. We's like brothers. We is brothers."

"Water under the bridge, Vinny. In fact, if you hadn't done that, I would have never been Zip Zilch, just Corey. And, by the way, Noford is not your only friend."

"I can't leave Noford and the bunch I'm in, but I promise I'll try to keep 'em from hurtin' you and your bunch."

"Thank you, Vinny Schmidt."

"Thank you, Corey Zilch."

He saluted and left.

36

SQUEAK

At Monday noon, Ferdy was Dr. Evil and I was Mini-Me. We sure did look funny in those bald caps and in those weird gray suits. The way those collars itched, I discovered, would put anybody in a foul mood. The two of us had practiced the evil laugh. We sounded really sick.

We stood at the door to greet our fellow students. Dr. Evil would say, "Welcome to my la-BOR-a-to-ry, lab-rats," then we would do the evil laugh thing.

They just stared at us. The trouble was that nobody had seen the *Austin Powers* movies, including Ferdy and I. This day had been my dad's contribution, and he loved those films, but it bombed at first. What saved us was the evil laugh. When we did it, everybody joined in. Then, when the cackles subsided, for some reason, the sound of *squeak, squeak, squeak* would resound through the room before they went back to what they were doing.

The Scuds simply watched, like they were studying us. We were ready to go change clothes when Chad stood, reached into his backpack, pulled out a gadget, fiddled with it, put it in his shirt pocket, put earphones on, and came up nose-to-nose

226

with Dr. Evil. Then Chad did the laugh. The room went silent.

"Heh, heh, heh. Do you know what this is?"

Dr. Evil's face turned flaming red.

Chad pulled Ferdy's iPod from his shirt.

"Old junk. Garbage. I think I'll toss it in the trash bin with the tofu slop."

"Give it back," Ferdy said, with his fists clenched. The murmuring in the room took word form— *"give it back, give it back, give it back."*

"Make me."

I could see the volcano was about to blow, so I shimmied between the two big guys. "Don't, Ferdy, don't. Think about Saturday's race."

"Sure, punk…" Chad tried to imitate my high voice, "Think about getting your be-hind beat. Why wait 'til Saturday? I'll do it right now."

I put my hands up on Ferdy's chest. "Don't let him pull you down with him, Ferdy. He's off the team. He can't win the race, so he doesn't want you to win it either."

By now, the Buds were surrounding Ferdy, and the Scuds were behind Chad. Noford clamped his ham-hands on Chad's shoulders, and ordered, "No, Chad. You do this thing and you lose your share of the swag."

"You ain't my boss," Chad said.

"Try me."

Ferdy turned to walk out the door. "Stick it," he said. Chad tried to follow, but both the Buds and the Scuds blocked the way.

That evening, as Noford was loading Vinny's gear into his Pop's Blazer, and Vinny came down to say goodbye, I told him why that old iPod meant so much to Ferdy.

"His father's, huh? Okay."

ooo

Tuesday, we were the Addams Family. Everybody thinks the Addams Family is cool. The lunchroom menu board said, "basil tomato bean stew." Hu snuck over and changed it to say, "bat meat stew." More people tried it than usual.

I was the oily Gomez with a striped suit and slicked back hair. Justine was a deliciously spooky Morticia. Ferdy was a scary Lurch, Hu was Uncle Festus, Shelly was Wednesday, and Sarah, in a fuzzy gray wig, was Grandmama. Sarah even looks good as an old lady.

This time we lined up just inside the door, greeting the kids as they came in with words like, "Welcome to our lair," and, "How does your blood feel today?" The more clever ones would ask things like, "How's It?" and, "Where's Pugsley?" For some strange reason, though, whenever they would reach me at the end of the row, they would just go, "squeak, squeak, squeak."

Netflix had made the Addams Family popular again, so every so often the crowd would strike up the song. Principal Farraday looked in twice, but only smiled and went back to his Merriam-Webster.

The odd thing was that the Scuds were not at their table. Finally, when we were about to leave, they entered together and Noford pushed Chad forward. He had a swollen lip and an eye turning blue. He approached Lurch, who took a step back. Chad mumbled "sorry" and handed Ferdy the stolen iPod.

Lurch grunted.

Now it was clear to everyone there which Scud was the bull moose who ruled the herd. Noford gave me a nod and led the Scuds to their table.

The crowd, on the other hand, chanted, *"Squeak, squeak, squeak."*

A while later, as my Buds were leaving to become themselves again, Vinny sidled up to me and whispered, "What'er you guys gonna be tomorrow?"

"Men in Black," I answered.

That night I said goodbye to my mouse friends in the basement. Some of them had learned not to take Dad's bait, and I had named them. I learned the survival of the species in real life. But I left them so I could move back to my own room to sleep in my own bed.

Then my dad and I took the Addams costumes back to Jimmy's house to exchange for two Men in Black suits. "Funny thing," Jimmy's mom said, "we've had a run on those. All I have left are two kid sizes."

"That will work," I said. "Hu and I are kid size."

ꙮ

On Wednesday Hu and I wore black suits, white shirts, black ties, floor length coats and, of course, sunglasses. I was a kid-sized Tommy Lee Jones, and Hu was a miniature Will Smith.

We took up our station at the door. A minute later, six more Men in Black, all sizes, filed in, making a row of eight. The crowd went crazy. The principal came out to see what was going on and went away smiling.

The Scuds were friendly, which shocked everybody. Had aliens taken over their bodies? I was last in line, and when the kids got to me, they would go *"squeak."* During a lull, I asked

229

Vinny, "What's with the squeaks?"

"Dude, you still don't get it, do ya. They're sayin' they know you's the Mole."

After Hu and I sat down at the Buds table in our suits, I realized I was hot. Finally, the school furnace was fixed. I started to take the coat off, but Sarah said, "You look good like that." So, I put it back on and sweated.

A weird thing started happening that day. Kids I didn't know came up to tell me things, like, "the girl's room stinks," and, "I don't have time between classes to get to my locker for the next class's books." I was the school complaint department.

"What's going on?" I asked Hu.

"You really *are* thick-headed, Corey. They are telling you things that they want you to pass on to Principal Farraday. They trust you."

"Oh."

When I got to the office he wasn't in, but the Vice Principal was there, so I told her what I had been told. She thanked me. On the way out, Noford blocked my path.

"Tomorrow, we do Men in Black again."

I said, "Whatever."

ooo

The next day, Hu and I were back in costume on our way to our station when Mr. Farraday nabbed us both.

"Terminated," he declared.

"Huh?"

"A treaty has been transacted, so your toil is truncated." I guess the principal had reached the letter "t."

I said, "Sir, could you use plain English. I don't think my friend understands you."

"Yes, I can. Zilch, you are fired."

230

Wow. Just like that, just when it started being fun. I stuttered, "B-b-but why?"

"Face it, boy. You were never very good at spying. I have found a better agent. This Noford Hammond boy is a born leader. He knows everything that is going on in the school."

He was right about that. In fact, Noford caused most of what was going on.

"He also has a fine cadre of subordinate associates who will supplement his efforts. Finally, I will be relieved of the burden of supervising student affairs."

Actually, I was relieved, too. Apparently "s" was a slippery slope, and he slid backward into it. I did not want to be in Principal Farraday's office when he reached the xyz's. That would be painful. However, I was still concerned about two things.

"Sir, I can still compete in sports, can't I?"

"Certainly, Zilch. You have earned that right."

"Thank you, Sir. One other thing. Students sometimes tell me things they want me to tell you. Could I still pass those concerns on to you?"

"Why, Zilch, maybe I underestimated you. Yes, you may have my ear. You are the first student in twenty-five years who asked for it. However, if this is a ploy to retain your position as my agent, the decision is final."

Hu had been silent in the office, but in the hallway, he said, "I had no idea what you have had to put up with."

The next day, in plain clothes, I watched the Men in Black closely. By the end of lunch hour, I thought I knew their game. Not only were the pockets of their long coats stuffed with contraband for sale, but they seemed to be holding some kind of raffle or sweepstakes or something. The candy bars were not just contraband, they were tickets, but I couldn't figure out what they were betting on.

37

CHARIOTS OF FIRE

oach Rusk pushed us hard that week to get us ready for the Conference Cross Country Championship Meet in Sumac. While we did warmups, he went down the line with encouraging words for each of us, telling us where he saw improvement, bringing up examples of our courage, telling us how much we meant to him, and praising us for working together as a team.

Then he sent us through our Butterworth Trail twice, without stopping, to build our endurance. Finally, we did wind sprints to prove we still had a kick after a long run.

On Thursday, he arranged a bus to take us to Sumac, five miles from our school, where Saturday's race would be held, and we ran that course twice so we could get used to the longer but smoother trail. Betty Jean's biker dad brought submarine sandwiches for us to eat in the grandstands after we ran. Coach announced that we wouldn't have practice on Friday. Instead, he invited us to his apartment for dinner and a movie. He wanted us to have, "fresh legs and a joyful heart" Saturday morning.

I didn't get home until dark. My family had eaten already, and they were in the living room watching *Wheel of Fortune.* That's when I told them I had been fired by Principal Farraday. They tried to comfort me until they realized I was happy about it.

Mom said, "This calls for a party!"

She brought out a big tub of ice cream, bananas, whip cream from a can, and other toppings, so we could make our own banana splits. Sis drenched hers in chocolate, Dad used maple syrup, Mom chose strawberry, and I went nuts. Good thing I wasn't running again until Saturday.

As we satisfied our sweet teeth, Mom said, "Corey, you must feel relieved."

"Oh yeah," I said, "I could do a dance."

"Please don't," my sister pleaded.

I went on, "I just have one problem left."

"What's that?" Dad asked.

"Saturday."

"What's the problem? Just go out there and win it like you did last year."

I told them what Ferdy and I had been doing, about the iPod, the music, and his father—everything. "I'm confused about what to do if our strategy works and I could still outrun him. Should I let him win?"

Sis said, "That would be nice of you."

Mom said, "Yes, that would be sweet."

"No, it wouldn't," Dad said. "That would be a hollow victory. He would know you did it, and your friendship would suffer. Letting him win would be dishonest. Honesty is the only policy, Son."

Sis said, "Somebody else will probably beat you both anyway."

"Yeah, could be," I said, "but the problem is the word 'beat.' I want to win, but I don't want to beat Ferdy, or anyone else either. If either one of us wins, it has to be fair and square."

"You've got the square part down. You might even be rectangular," Sis said.

"You really are growing up," my dad said, "now that you can tell the difference it makes in *how* you win. Sportsmanship is about winning, not beating. The point is not to humiliate the other team, but for both of you to do your best, so talent and effort can rise to the top. Then everybody can feel good about it."

What had happened to my father, anyway, that he got so much wiser over the past year? But, on the other hand, we still wear those bright orange sweat suits.

Dad wasn't done with his pep talk. He added, "A true friend gets as much satisfaction out of seeing his friend win as he would out of winning himself."

ⓞⓞⓞ

Coach Rusk's apartment is a dump—with warn carpet, scratched woodwork, stained paint, and pipes that clank. I guess youth pastors don't make much money. He had only a sofa and a TV in his living room, and he told the boys to let the girls have the sofa. The boys sat on blankets he spread over the carpet. Our supper was hot dogs, macaroni and cheese, potato chips, Oreos, and water. During the movie he made popcorn in a kettle on the stove and gave us our choice of orange soda or grape Kool-Aid.

He did have a decent flat screen TV on the wall, wired to an ancient VCR on the floor. From a box of videotapes, he pulled one and slid it in. *Hum-hum-click-hum. Pause.*

Coach explained, "This is my favorite movie of all time. I wanted you to see it before the race tomorrow. The movie is old, 1981, based on a true story that is even older, 1924, when the Olympics was in Paris. I know, I know, you're wondering what could be interesting that happened before even your grandfather was born. But give it a chance. The movie won the Academy Award for best picture, and it's about running. They call it *Chariots of Fire.*

As a history buff, I was fascinated. A movie about running, really? A true story? At first most of the team was restless, getting up for popcorn, or to use the bathroom, but by the middle no one was moving. By the end we were, like, "Let's go run our race now."

The one thing that Eric Liddell said that stuck in my head permanently was, "I believe that God made me for a purpose. But He also made me fast, and when I run, I feel His pleasure."

Wow.

000

The starting time was ten o'clock Saturday morning. Coach told us to be there at nine. All the Buds, including Sarah and Hu, were there by eight-thirty. Sarah brought a blanket, spread it on the side of the levee, and we sat in a huddle in the cool damp air. The four of us who had seen the movie told Sarah and Hu all about it. Coach was there getting ready, talking with the officials, greeting the other coaches and teams as they arrived.

Before things got busy, he came over to sit with us a short time. He accessed his Bible app on his phone and read this to us: *"They that wait upon the Lord shall renew their strength; they shall mount up on wings as eagles; they shall run, and not be weary..."*

Because this was youth group, not the team, he could pray with us without getting in trouble. Before he went back to his duties, we all linked arms, and he prayed for us to rise up like eagles. Pastor Rusk left, and we lay back on the side of the hill staring at cloud shapes. Ferdy listened to all the songs that were in his strategy on his iPod.

When the other team members arrived, we did our stretching and warm-ups. As Ferdy and I stretched side-by-side, I told him, "I want you to win, Ferdy, but I don't want me to lose."

He grinned and said, "What makes you think you've got a chance?"

"If somebody else can beat us fair and square, that would be okay. But if it's just the two of us, you will have to win it on your own, because I will refuse to lose."

He said, "Either way we will both be winners."

"Exactly."

The starting line was long and divided into segments. Our area was decided by the coaches drawing numbers from a hat. This time our team got the worst position, at the outside end. However, we were not intimidated. *Chariots of Fire* was still on our minds.

38

THE FLAME

The ground was soft from rain the night before, but the Sumac track was built well. Coach led our team through, jogging, pointing out potential trouble spots. The race would be twice around, longer than our middle school trail, but shorter than the high school course. He showed us markers to measure our progress and suggested the best places to make a move.

Unlike our woodsy Butterworth trail, nearly the whole Sumac track is visible to the fans in the bleachers. Only one corner, behind an elevated golf green and another corner through a grove of bald sumac and burr oak that still held their brown leaves, were hidden from sight. Those sumacs, with raspberry bushes under them, were where Chad had knocked Cherise out of last year's race.

The sky was overcast, but warmer, about fifty degrees. We all wore our own sweatshirts, mine was orange. Each team would wear outer vests of a different color with numbers for ID.

As my team jogged past the parking lot, I saw my family arrive in the "pumpkin-mobile." My dad had junked his rusty old Durango and replaced it with a used orange mini-van so the whole family of six could ride together in style.

When coach gave us twenty minutes free time, I trotted over to my family—Dad, Mom, Kitty, Annie, and even my stylish sister—decked out in orange. That gave me a warm glow.

The smart fans had brought towels to wipe with and blankets to sit on. Dad brought a plastic tarp, orange, of course, big enough for two families and laid it up the side of the levee next to the tarp that Betty Jean's biker dad brought that could have held half of Hanway. Sarah rolled up her now soggy blanket, and she and Hu moved to my family's tarp.

A little way down the sidelines, at the end of a dirt lane, was an ancient Suburban with the two hinged doors in the back wide open, surrounded by people. I wandered down for a look.

The Scuds were running a concession stand. The sign on the left door said:

Five dollars for a candy bar? That couldn't be right. The adults shook their heads at that and settled for coffee, but the students were forking over fives for candy. Not me. My father would say, "I kid you not," this is how the sign on the right door read:

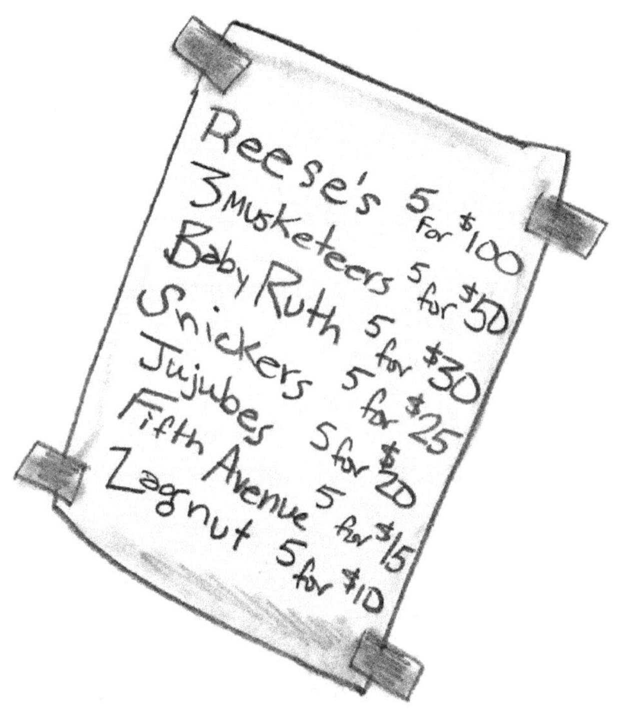

Crazy! Reese's are good, but would anyone pay a hundred dollars for five of them, when they could buy one for five dollars? And why would anybody pay five for one Zagnut when they could buy five for 10 dollars, then resell them for a profit? I was amazed the Scuds could be that dumb.

But I guess Jimmy was dumber than I thought. He and Sis came over to buy a Fifth Avenue for him and a Zagnut for her. What is a Zagnut anyway?

Weirder yet, even though trash cans were everywhere, the kids would eat the candy and stuff the wrappers in their pockets. At least they didn't throw them on the ground.

On the way back I saw Ferdy's mom sitting with my mom. Kitty was wrapped up tight in a parka, watching Annie in a snowsuit climb up and slide down the slippery bank. Harley and his dad—Justine's dad—were talking with mine. Sarah and Hu were sitting with Sarah's mother and sister on our tarp. Hu's parents could never come to anything because of the restaurant. Shelly's parents were by themselves in the grandstand.

At nine-forty-five, the team gathered at our starting box. Stretch, bend, stretch, bend, run in place knees high, we moved as a team. Then we huddled with Coach for the pep-talk.

"Today is our last time together as a team so make the most of it. Eighth graders, this is your chance to shine. Next year you will start at the bottom rung again, running with Seniors even, climbing the ladder to success. The girls and guys will be separate teams next year, so you will need to find other ways to see each other."

Coach paused then to wink for some reason.

"The high school coaches are here today, and it's okay to show off for them. I am proud of every one of you. We had a good year, you worked hard, you learned how to run, you supported each other, and you put your heart into winning as a team. As a result, we are tied with Pennington for the league lead. We can win the title today.

"Sixth and seventh graders, you have wonderful potential. Keep running every day until we meet again next summer, so we can celebrate more victories.

"As for this race, relax and enjoy the experience. Let your body memory take over, run in rhythm, set the pace that feels right, and save just enough for a final kick. The rain has left some soft spots which, if you land on your heels, could cause you to skid. Remember—ball, heel, ball, push. When you reach the grove the second time, assess how much you have left, and use it all by the finish.

"Now, hands together, one minute of silence."

Whatever the others were using their minute for, I used mine to pray, for me, my team, and, especially, for my friend Ferdy. Then Coach whispered, "Amen," and we did our chant: *"Hanway Hamsters, all for one, one for all! GO TEAM!"*

On purpose, Ferdy and I took the spots on the very end. Seventy-five runners make a traffic jam, and at my size I get lost in crowds. Our plan was for me to sprint down the sideline with Ferdy close behind, so we could run side by side in the front. If the traffic closed in too soon Ferdy would lead, since at his height he could see the best path to the front. We aimed to stay together and help each other the whole race.

Leaning over to look down the long curved starting line, I waved to Shelly and Justine, who also planned to run in tandem. Rochester was the next team, with Bossie staring back at me. The face on the tattoo, which I had never seen standing still before, was not a sister or mother or girlfriend, but a cow.

Oh.

Pennington's stable was led by a smaller version of last year's racehorse. I barely beat him. This must be a brother. As the referee raised the starting pistol, the horse raised his front hoof, ah, hand, imitated a gun, and shot me. No time to look farther down the row.

All went quiet except for Ferdy, humming.

Ready!

Under his breath Ferdy sang, *"Hey, hey, hey, you've got me all wound up and ready to go…"*

Set!

"…Where have you been all my life? Why did you wait so long?"

Bang!

Stampede. Like a calf without horns trying to stay ahead in the running of the bulls, I galloped down the edge of the chaos toward the clearing ahead. The racehorse stepped in front of me, veering into my path when I tried to pass. Ferdy-to-the-rescue stepped up even with the horse so I could drop behind and run behind him until we were past.

"Bang, bang," neighed the Pennington runner, shooting again with his finger. I had thought that the cowboys, not their horses, shot guns.

Finally, after about a hundred yards, we were in the lead and could settle into our pace.

The racehorse and the long-haired blonde from Whitmore were close behind. We sped along at a comfortable clip until Ferdy switched songs on his internal iPod.

"...*Every time I got to thinking, where'd they disappear?*"

We rounded the corner behind the golf green, and once we got back on the straightaway, we could see the stragglers who hadn't reached the turn. This long, flat stretch was good for a steady beat. Trouble was, I couldn't step with the same beat as Ferdy, because with my short legs I would fall behind. I had to return to *Gilligan's Island* and play that theme song in my head.

As planned, at the oak grove, Ferdy changed music to preserve some strength for the second round. I was grateful.

"...*The dream police, they live inside of my head...*"

The first one to pass us was Bossie, puffing, but plowing ahead. I resisted the urge to moo.

Next, goldilocks—*What was her name?*—from Whitmore glided smoothly by, her long ponytail swinging side to side.

Racehorse Junior rode by with another bang-bang.

Then Justine and Shelly pulled alongside. Shelly whispered, "Don't rest too long. The crowd is watching." I nodded thanks as they passed.

Just as we reached the steep hill where we ran up the

levee, J.D. from Fogtown caught us on the right side, which meant he had to go higher up the levee on the curve at the top. We had to slow because the rut that most of the runners followed was slick. J.D.'s footing was solid and he sailed past on the downhill.

As Ferdy and I attempted to get back into rhythm, a voice just behind me said, "Hi, Corey. Hi, Ferdy. I caught you. I'm fast, too, like you. Let's win this race, huh, huh?"

Yeesh. How can Ferdy sing and Rory talk while they're running? I can barely grunt.

That's when, near the grandstand, Ferdy sang, "*the dream police, they're coming to arrest me, oh no…*" and almost stopped.

Suddenly, Ferdy changed his mental CD.

"*…Don't just sit there with your head in your hands…*" He charged ahead, with a growling voice. "*…Get up, get up, get on the ball…*"

Ferdy pounded the cinders, I pecked them. We left Rory with his chatter and caught J.D. in front of my family's tarp, to their applause. Next, we passed Bossie before the golf green.

When we drew even with our girl Buds, I grunted, "Sorry…but…"

Justine answered, "Go for it!"

Only the blonde and the racehorse were ahead.

Ferdy switched to his fastest tune: "*…didn't I, didn't I, didn 't I see you cryin'?…*"

That song hit me. That was me before the Buds. The same thought must have come to Ferdy, too, since he grinned at me. This was the fastest pace before the sprint. We blazed by the racehorse in the oak grove. I couldn't help myself. I went, "Bang, bang."

That left blondie—goldilocks—Gloria. *That's it, Gloria!* Wow, she was good—smooth, strong, determined.

As we approached the berm up the levee, I

243

croaked to Ferdy, "Take the high side."

The inside rut was now muddy from all the feet smearing it. When I tried to jump the worst spot, I slid a yard or so. By the time I righted myself, Ferdy was three strides ahead of me and three strides behind Gloria. I knew I couldn't catch either one at this pace.

I yelled to Ferdy, "The Flame!"

Lightening couldn't have been more dramatic. He threw back his shoulders and bellowed, "...*Wherever you go, I'll be with you...*"

Gloria turned her head in time to see Ferdy go into double-time, pump his arms, and fly by like he had a jet pack on.

"*...Remember, after the fire, after all the rain, I will be the flame...*"

Both of us watched in awe as he spread both arms out ahead of him, burst the tape at the finish line, and roared, "I will be the flame!"

The whole crowd watched in shock as he wrapped his arms around himself and collapsed on the ground. Coach rushed over and held up his head. He was crying. He was okay, though.

I finished third and ran right up to him. He looked at me— no—more like *through* me, into the sky, and said, "Did you see him, Zip? He was right here, standing tall, holding his light high."

"Who was?"

"My father! When I hugged him, he disappeared, but he was here."

Coach and I helped Ferdy up and walked him down the chute where the judge gave him number one, Gloria number two, and me number three. Racehorse got fourth, and Shelly and Justine tied for fifth. Even Rory finished number fifteen. Hanway won by a mudslide.

Candy wrappers were flying everywhere. Did they save

them for confetti? Kids were pulling them out of their pockets and throwing them with disgust.

Someone hit me in the gut with an unopened Zagnut. I picked it up and looked at it. Suddenly I looked around for Principal Farraday, remembering how all my troubles started the last time I grabbed a candy bar. But this was not Hanway School, so he had no power here to suspend people. I picked up the wrappers that blew my way. The only wrappers I didn't see were Fifth Avenue's.

A stream of people, including Jimmy, was flowing to the Scuds' stand, turning in Fifth Avenue wrappers and walking away with money. I stared at the Zagnut.

5 for 10—Zagnut—Z—Zip Zilch.

5 for 15—Fifth Avenue—F—Ferdy Phillips.

Another Zagnut hit me, along with what it meant.

The first letter of each candy matched the first letter of a name on our team. The 5-fors were not prices. They were odds. The Scuds were running a gambling business.

Chad knew all the runners and he had set the odds. I felt good that he had rated me most likely to win, but now I had people mad at me, throwing Zagnuts. Oh well, I might as well get used to not making everybody happy. I ripped open the one in my hand and took a bite. Not bad.

Annie escaped from Kitty, scampering over to hug my leg. "Zippy, Zippy, Zippy, I love you!"

How could anybody feel bad after that?!

The announcer belted out the race results.

"Congratulations, to the Hanway Middle School Hamsters, repeat Conference Champions! Special kudos to two great

The Whitmore Whippets cheered and hugged Gloria but were drowned out by the Hanway crowd. The high school football team, led by Jimmy Smithers, hoisted Ferdy on their shoulders and began chanting, *"Fer-dy, Fer-dy, Fer-dy, Fer-dy ..."*

You will think I'm crazy, and maybe I am, but I will swear I heard it. Above all the chanting, I heard two voices, female and male, crying out triumphantly, "THAT'S MY BOY! THAT'S MY SON!"

I felt even better than I had a year ago.

We won!

HANWAY
M.S.
H
EST.1991

A Little Something About the Author

Paul Maitland might look like somebody's kind ol' grandpa, but his heart burns young and is full to the rim with middle school stories that he yearns to share with the readers of the world.

Paul grew up to be a church pastor, which he enjoyed very much. In that job, he was able to work with children in many capacities. Upon retirement, he settled into a chair and began to let a life's worth of stories out of his heart and onto the page. His *Zip Zilch: Nobody's a Nuthin' Series* is only the beginning.

Follow Paul Maitland on Amazon (click the button under the book's image on any Amazon.com retail page), and they will email you every time a new book comes out by this fantastic author.

Books by Paul (so far)…

Zip Zilch: Nobody's a Nuthin' Book One

Buds & Scuds: Nobody's a Nuthin' Book Two

Boys with Tales: 25 Character-building Tales for Boys and the Adults Who Love Them

Mr. Maitland has also written a fantastic and fun book for Dads and Sons *(or boys and their chosen mentor/adult)* to enjoy together!

Look for it TODAY on Amazon.com in paperback, hardcover and Kindle ebook!

Little Roni Publishers

LOVES Middle Grade Novels.

Here are some fun reads from our other authors: